100 DAYS TO
FREEDOM

from
Anger

Daily Devotional

STEPHEN ARTERBURN

AspirePress

100 DAYS TO FREEDOM FROM ANGER

Copyright © 2021 Stephen Arterburn
Published by Aspire Press
An imprint of Tyndale House Ministries
Carol Stream, Illinois
www.hendricksonrose.com

ISBN: 978-162862-998-9

The views and opinions expressed in this book are those of the author(s) and do not necessarily express the views of Tyndale House Ministries or Aspire Press, nor is this book intended to be a substitute for mental health treatment or professional counseling. The information in this resource is intended as guidelines for healthy living. Please consult qualified medical, legal, pastoral, and psychological professionals regarding individual concerns.

Written with Becky Brown

Book design by Sergio Urquiza

Printed by APS
October 2021, 1st Printing

This book is given to

_____

on this day

_____

Contents

Introduction

Peace can be a scarce commodity in these turbulent times. Jesus said, "I have told you these things, so that in me you may have peace. In this world you will have trouble. But take heart! I have overcome the world" (John 16:33). So how can you find the genuine peace that Jesus described? By making God a full partner in every aspect of your life, that's how.

On the pages that follow, you'll be asked to spend a few minutes each day thinking about ways that you and God, working together, can overcome your challenges, organize your life, prioritize your duties, redirect your thoughts, and follow the path that your heavenly Father intends for you to take. When you do these things, you'll receive the peace and the spiritual abundance that can, and should, be yours. So for the next 100 days, please try this experiment: read a chapter a day and internalize the ideas that you find here.

This text contains biblically based prescriptions for the inevitable challenges of tough times. As you consider your own circumstances, remember this: whatever the size of your problems, God is bigger. Much bigger. He will instruct you, protect you, energize you, and heal you, if you let him. So let him. Pray fervently, listen carefully, work diligently, and treat every single day as an exercise in spiritual growth because that's precisely what every day can be—and will be—if you learn how to let God help you rise above the challenges of these turbulent times and experience true peace.

Day 1

Quit It!

Stop being angry! Turn from your rage!
Do not lose your temper—it only leads to harm.

Psalm 37:8 NLT

If it were only so easy to not be angry. Usually, that requires everything in your life to cooperate in the way you expect and for the people in your life to be agreeable to your demands. That sounds a bit much when you say it out loud, but in your mind that is pretty much what is expected.

Anger is a reaction to a circumstance that is unexpected. It is an expression of our internal pain, fear, sorrow, anxiety, weakness, and many other emotions. Anger gives the illusion of control or power in a situation in which we don't feel we have either.

Think about the last time you lost your temper. What was happening? Was the circumstance something you had either control or power over? Were you surprised by your expression of anger—like it was a bit over the top? When you start seeing the negative impact of your anger, you can take the opportunity to replace the reaction with positive and helpful responses.

The idea that you should never be angry is not realistic. You cannot "quit" anger—rather, you can stop the force that unhealthy anger can create in your life.

How much more grievous are the consequences of anger than the causes of it.

Marcus Aurelius

A wise man looks for everything inside of himself; a madman seeks for everything in others.

Confucius

We all have negative urges, but we don't have to act out those urges.

Fred Rogers

For Further Reflection

James 1:14-25; Psalm 37:3-13; Colossians 3:1-11

TODAY'S PRAYER

Heavenly Father, help me as I seek to understand the anger within me. Reveal what I need to heal and what needs to be removed. I need your help to resolve this and to use my life for your will. Thank you for your grace! Amen.

Day 2

Anger Management

People with understanding control their anger;
a hot temper shows great foolishness.

Proverbs 14:29 NLT

You may have heard the phrase "anger management" before. The phrase is somewhat of a misnomer, because the goal is not simply managing anger when the feelings arise but dealing with what is creating the anger. That is where control comes in.

Many people think that the idea that we have control in our lives is an illusion. However, you do control many things in your life. For example, you probably aren't lashing out at your boss or your pastor (hopefully!). We can stop rage almost instantly depending on the target. We might lash out at the driver in the next lane, and then pull into the church parking lot with a smile on our face.

Scripture indicates that the evidence of "great foolishness" is a "hot temper." Learning to control anger isn't about suppressing the emotion, which can actually fuel the flames. Understanding what drives your anger is the key to controlling your anger. There are ways to express anger without creating more problems. Understanding where the emotional reaction is coming from can also provide insight to a solution.

Remember, the goal isn't to manage anger; it is to understand and control what drives the powerful emotion, using it for good. After all, does anyone want to be viewed as a fool?

Hot heads and cold hearts never solved anything.

Billy Graham

Do not say, "I cannot help having a bad temper." Friend, you must help it. Pray to God to help you overcome it at once, for either you must kill it, or it will kill you. You cannot carry a bad temper into heaven.

Charles Spurgeon

Make no mistake: Satan's specialty is psychological warfare. If he can turn us on God ("It's not fair!") or turn us on others ("It's their fault!") or turn us on ourselves ("I'm so stupid!"), we won't turn on him. If we keep fighting within ourselves and losing our own inner battles, we'll never have the strength to stand up and fight our true enemy.

Beth Moore

For Further Reflection

Ephesians 4:29–32; Romans 12:17–21;
James 1:19–21

TODAY'S PRAYER

Lord Jesus, I want to grow in understanding and wisdom so I can serve you and be the person you created me to be. Through the power of your Holy Spirit working in me, help me have self-control and to not be governed by anger. In your name I pray, Amen.

Day 3

Anger Rules

And don't sin by letting anger control you.
Don't let the sun go down while you are still angry,
for anger gives a foothold to the devil.

Ephesians 4:26–27 NLT

D o you ever feel out of control in your anger? As though a force within compels you to unleash whatever feeling is suppressed? That's because anger does, in fact, come from within. You might feel like anger stems from something that happened or a person who "pushed your buttons," yet it's something much deeper.

Consider this object lesson: If a person holds a glass of milk and their arm gets bumped, why does the milk come out of the glass? The typical answer is "because their arm got bumped." But milk comes out of the glass because that is what was in the glass. What comes out of us when we're bumped is what is inside us.

Comedian Phyllis Diller wrote in her 1966 book *Phyllis Diller's Housekeeping Hints*, "Never go to bed angry. Stay up and fight." Although we might find the quote humorous, it is not the best advice, because when anger is the driving force, rational thinking is greatly diminished.

If anger is ruling your life, discover where it is rooted. You may not realize how many times the sun has set on your anger because you stuffed it down inside of you. Begin to explore—maybe through journaling—how you feel when you are angry. It could be working with a counselor to unpack what has been stored. Clear up what is inside and begin to experience life where peace rules.

———————▲———————

We may not be able to prevent other people from being our enemies, but we can prevent ourselves from being enemies toward others.

Warren Wiersbe

Holding anger and angry thoughts doesn't allow love to grow in your heart. If you don't have love in your heart or mind, your actions will not come from a place of compassion or kindness.

Winnie Anderson

Whatever is making you so angry, it's time for you to give it to God and get over it.

Joyce Meyer

———————▲———————

For Further Reflection

Colossians 3:15; Psalm 51:7–12; Ecclesiastes 7:9

TODAY'S PRAYER

Lord, you know me better than I know myself. Clean my heart and mind of the things that are not of you. Forgive me, heal me and make me whole. Thank you for your grace and mercy at work in my life. Amen.

Day 4

Free from Anger

*In every place of worship, I want men to pray with holy
hands lifted up to God, free from anger and controversy.*

1 TIMOTHY 2:8

I f you are a follower of Jesus, worship is part of your life—
and it isn't just reserved for a church building. Worship
can take place in your car as you listen to a song that
touches your soul, or it can be out in nature taking in the
beauty. True worship that is focused on God is a powerful
experience!

Apostle Paul, the writer of 1 Timothy, emphasized how
worship can be interrupted by anger and controversy.
Even in the early church period, worship had distractions!
Nowadays, so many things fight for our attention, including
our own thoughts and feelings, making true, focused worship
a challenge.

It's difficult to pray when angry. Anger consumes us as we
replay what happened, rehearse what we will do or say, and
obsess over the wrong that occurred. When we have been
offended, wronged, or hurt, anger is expected. What we do
with the anger is so very important. Anger turned inward
can imprison us. To resolve anger, we must understand and
express it.

Freedom in worship is experienced when we surrender the
injustices, wounds, and offenses we have experienced to
Jesus. As we allow the Lord to provide healing, we begin to

have a deeper relationship with him, one that is free from anger and free to worship.

————————◢————————

When we are in touch with God's joy and peace in us, then we become whole and holy persons. Like living torches, we radiate the light and heat of God's compassionate love.

Mark Yaconelli

As a Christian, you can enjoy life because your conscience is clear. You can enjoy life because you are secure within God's love.

Rick Warren

Even if people have disappointed you or circumstances have not turned out as you had hoped or prayed, know that God is with you, cares for you, and loves you. He is working all these things together for your good right at this very moment.

Christine Caine

————————◢————————

For Further Reflection
Mark 11:22–25; 1 Peter 5:6–10; Psalm 71:19–24

TODAY'S PRAYER
Thank you, Lord for the freedom you provide! Help me to release the bitterness, pain, and resentment to you. Begin your healing work so that I may worship you only. Amen.

Grace and Mercy

They refused to obey and did not remember the miracles
you had done for them. Instead, they became stubborn
and appointed a leader to take them back to their slavery
in Egypt. But you are a God of forgiveness, gracious
and merciful, slow to become angry, and rich in
unfailing love. You did not abandon them.

NEHEMIAH 9:17

Anger can create a type of amnesia, where we forget that we have made mistakes and require patience from others. When we're quick to react in anger, we fail to recall times we've received latitude and grace from others for our imperfections. We become stubborn and refuse to listen to reason and more importantly, truth.

Self-awareness can help us remember our own weaknesses. As we work to understand what is driving the anger and resentment, we can strive to be more mindful and present. When someone doesn't meet our expectations, we can address the issue, not attack the person. When circumstances don't go the way we want, we can choose not to let disappointment cause us to react negatively. We can choose not to live in a reactive state of mind.

Even in situations in which anger is justified, if we don't work on healing the wound, bitterness will creep in, keeping us stuck in the past, forgetting that we have a present and a future of hope.

Anger creates difficulties in relationships, feeds bitterness, and allows shame to take over our lives. But God is full of grace and mercy, forgiveness, and love for us. We can begin today to resolve the anger that has been dominating our lives. God doesn't want us to live one more day driven by the things that once enslaved us.

Anger and bitterness are two noticeable signs of being focused on self and not trusting God's sovereignty in your life. When you believe that God causes all things to work together for good to those who belong to him and love him, you can respond to trials with joy instead of anger or bitterness.

John C. Broger

Feelings are indicators, not dictators. They can indicate where your heart is in the moment, but that doesn't mean they have the right to dictate your behavior and boss you around. You are more than the sum total of your feelings and perfectly capable of that little gift … called self-control.

Lysa TerKeurst

For Further Reflection
Micah 7:7–10, 18; Psalm 86:1–7; Psalm 145:8

TODAY'S PRAYER
Father God, today I ask forgiveness for the times that anger has driven me to be harsh and bitter. Help me as I forgive others and learn to have patience with this imperfect world trusting that you are in control. Amen.

Day 6

Family Tradition

*The Lord is slow to anger and filled with unfailing love,
forgiving every kind of sin and rebellion. But he does not
excuse the guilty. He lays the sins of the parents upon
their children; the entire family is affected—even
children in the third and fourth generations.*

NUMBERS 14:18

What was your home like when you were growing up?
Was it a peaceful home where everyone was loving
and kind to one another? Or was it more like a war
zone where you were making sure to stay out of target range and
careful not to set off a land mine? Family life can be challenging
when someone in the home is angry and reactive.

Many times, people's views of God are shaped by family
experiences. If you had an angry parent, it could influence
the way you approach God, thinking he also is angry and
short tempered. Many times, these family influences have
been generations in the making. Without realizing there was
a problem with the relationships in the family, people carry
the behavior patterns to the next generation.

Think about your current home life and family. Is the
atmosphere similar to the one you grew up in? And if so, is
that a good thing? You can make changes to create a home
and family that reflects the nature of God—slow to anger,
filled with unfailing love, and forgiving.

What can you do today to create a new family tradition that is closer to the version of God's plan? It could be forgiving someone who hurt you instead of maintaining the hurt they caused. Maybe it's keeping your criticism out of conversations with your loved ones. It might be keeping control of your reactions. Even if you live alone, you might be carrying anger into your relationships. Choose to do whatever you can to create a peaceful home and create a new family tradition.

If you and I want to stir up a resentment tomorrow that may rankle across the decades and endure until death, just let us indulge in a little stinging criticism—no matter how certain we are that it is justified.

Dale Carnegie

If you want the great and mighty things God has for you, you must get to the root of anger and deal with it. Get rid of the masks and face the things that happened in your life that made you the way you are today. Admit that you can't change by yourself. Until the root is removed, it'll continue to produce one bad fruit after another.

Joyce Meyer

For Further Reflection
Psalm 133:1; Colossians 3:13-15; 1 Peter 4:8-10

TODAY'S PRAYER
Jesus, thank you for your forgiveness. Help me to offer it to my family and loved ones. Create a godly home for me and those I love as I follow your path. Amen.

Day 7

Instructions for Life

Understand this, my dear brothers and sisters:
You must all be quick to listen, slow to speak,
and slow to get angry. Human anger does not
produce the righteousness God desires.

JAMES 1:19–20

Many people like to do things without having a list of instructions, directions, maps, or someone in charge. Such individuals resist the idea of having someone else in control or having to conform to rules. But most of us like when other people follow directions and advice—especially directions and advice we're giving.

Instructions and rules are a basic part of life. Certain things work better when done a certain way. If we tend to be determined to do things our way—and get angry when we can't—we can encounter challenges in our lives. Willingness to learn and receive instruction are crucial to success.

Have you been told you are hard-headed, stubborn, or obstinate? Do you feel frustrated when you have to adhere to a certain way of doing things? Then you might need to adjust your thinking. You might have great ideas, intellect, and the ability to lead others to do great things. But if you are not teachable throughout your life, you will become angry or at the very least bitter—because life has rules and directions until your very last breath! Begin today by following the instructions in James 1:19–20 and experience the life God has for you.

Not being outraged by anything is a superpower.

James Pierce

Shouting something didn't make it any more possible.

Angie Sage

Anybody can become angry – that is easy, but to be angry with the right person and to the right degree and at the right time and for the right purpose, and in the right way – that is not within everybody's power and is not easy.

Aristotle

For Further Reflection

Proverbs 19:11; Psalm 34:11-14; 1 Timothy 2:1-4

TODAY'S PRAYER

Lord, I pray for a spirit of willingness. Help me to follow your leadership and to offer grace to those I am leading. Please give me discernment to use my gifts and talents to bring you glory in my life and to not frustrate and irritate others. In your name I ask, Amen.

Day 8

What's the Problem?

What is causing the quarrels and fights among you?
Don't they come from the evil desires at war within you?
You want what you don't have, so you scheme and kill
to get it. You are jealous of what others have, but you
can't get it, so you fight and wage war to take it away
from them. Yet you don't have what you want
because you don't ask God for it.

<small>James 4:1–2</small>

Sometimes we can't figure out how to get along with people. It feels like everyone is trying to complicate our lives. Maybe we feel like avoiding people altogether to get some peace.

Sometimes the difficulty lies in accepting that it's not always someone else's fault. If we believe there is always someone else to blame, we miss the opportunity to discover what is at the core of the issue. We will continue to find ourselves struggling to find contentment, connect in healthy relationships, and enjoy peace.

Not every battle that comes our way is one we have to fight. Some battles belong to the person bringing it into our lives; other battles are opportunities for us to learn patience.

When struggling with interpersonal conflict, start by asking God to reveal what is really going on. Ask him to reveal the truth about the situations that seem to be causing the issue. We can be vulnerable and honest with God about what (or whom) we are struggling with and seek to understand what might need to change inside us. Being defensive and reactive to everyone steals life and joy. Contentment and peace are found when we have deep connection with God.

If you spend your time hoping someone will suffer the consequences for what they did to your heart, then you're allowing them to hurt you a second time in your mind.

Shannon L. Alder

Anger is an acid that can do more harm to the vessel in which it is stored than to anything on which it is poured.

Mark Twain

Anger … It's a paralyzing emotion … you can't get anything done. People sort of think it's an interesting, passionate, and igniting feeling— I don't think it's any of that—it's helpless, it's absence of control.

Toni Morrison

For Further Reflection

1 Thessalonians 5:15–23; 1 Peter 3:8–11;
Matthew 11:28–30

TODAY'S PRAYER

Lord God, I desire your peace for my life instead of strife. Search my heart and show me the places where I need your wisdom and forgiveness. Thank you for your grace and mercy in my life and help me offer this to others. Amen.

Day 9

Route Guidance

So, I say, let the Holy Spirit guide your lives. Then you
won't be doing what your sinful nature craves.

GALATIANS 5:16

M any newer-model vehicles have a GPS or Global
Positioning System, which uses satellites to
help navigate to destinations. This has been a
revolutionary change in driving. Paper maps and atlases are
a rare find in any automobile today.

When we are followers of Jesus, we receive the Holy Spirit to
guide our lives. As we mature in our faith, we become aware
of changes in our values, our activities, and our relationships
that help us become more like Jesus. Anger and resentment
have less control over us. The Holy Spirit's guidance enables
us to experience the freedom that Jesus died for us to have.

Throughout our faith journey, we have to pay close attention
to our "map," the Bible, and learn what Jesus said about
relationships with people and God the Father, along with
serving and loving others. We learn about how we should live
and follow Christ. As we become more familiar with the text, we
will also become attuned to where the Holy Spirit leads us. We
will begin to recognize when we need to settle an issue, because
we will be prompted in our spirits to make it right. Our lives
begin to look different because of the Holy Spirit's working.

Look at the list of the fruit of the Spirit mentioned later in
Galatians 5, and see if you are heading in the right direction

or if you need to reroute your journey. The Holy Spirit's guidance in life is the best GPS you can have!

Having your spiritual radar up in constant anticipation of his presence—even in the midst of the joyful chaos and regular rhythms of your everyday living—is paramount in hearing God, because sometimes the place and manner you find Him is the least spectacular you'd expect.

Priscilla Shirer

If I can center down and strengthen the core of who I am, and the core of who I am is my relationship with God, then that helps me maintain peace deep down. If I can maintain a healthy spiritual core, I think that's enormous for helping the stress.

Anne Graham Lotz

God speaks through a variety of means. In the present God primarily speaks by the Holy Spirit, through the Bible, prayer, circumstances, and the church.

Henry Blackaby

For Further Reflection

Galatians 5:17-26; John 14:26; Romans 5:5-6

TODAY'S PRAYER

Thank you, Lord, for your gift of the Holy Spirit working and abiding in my life! Please give me the sensitivity to where the Holy Spirit is leading and guiding me, so that I may be more and more like you. Amen.

Designer Label

Control your temper, for anger labels you a fool.

ECCLESIASTES 7:9

"Hot head," "cantankerous," "testy," and "short-fused" are all labels we have used—or have perhaps been used on us—to describe a person known by their anger. Ecclesiastes 7:9 goes as far as to use the label "fool." That is a serious label. The definition for fool is a person who acts unwisely or imprudently; a silly person. Yet anger often makes a person feel powerful, certain, and "righteous" in whatever they are upset about.

If you recognize that you have been labeled by your anger, that's great, because the first step to change is awareness. You are heading in the right direction! Is your anger defining you in a way that is less than God's best for your life? Begin today by changing your label by surrendering to God your attitude, temper, and the emotions that lie underneath. Deciding to make a change in your life is never simple or easy, but it is worth doing.

Your label might have come from life experience. It could stem from a rough childhood or loss, or you might have been so wounded that you are reacting to anything or anyone that seems a threat. Today is the day to begin to accept the label that God gave you—loved, precious, and forgiven.

Other labels sometimes get attached along with anger, such as guilt and shame, but God is able to remove those and provide healing. Change and redemption is possible. What a great gift to receive—a new name!

———————▲———————

What they call you is one thing. What you answer to is something else.

Lucille Clifton

We cannot change our past ... we cannot change the fact that people will act in a certain way. We cannot change the inevitable. The only thing we can do is play on the one string we have, and that is our attitude. I am convinced that life is 10% what happens to me and 90% of how I react to it. And so, it is with you ... we are in charge of our attitudes.

Charles R. Swindoll

The most important decision you make is to be in a good mood.

Voltaire

———————▲———————

For Further Reflection
Matthew 5:21-24; 2 Peter 1:3-9; Psalm 119:1

TODAY'S PRAYER
Lord God, I desire to be known as your child,
to reflect you in my attitudes and relationships.
Forgive me for my sins and help me to recognize
that I am your beloved. In your name I ask, Amen.

Day 11

Why Are You So Angry?

"Why are you so angry?" the Lord asked Cain. "Why do you look so dejected? You will be accepted if you do what is right. But if you refuse to do what is right, then watch out! Sin is crouching at the door, eager to control you. But you must subdue it and be its master."

GENESIS 4:6–7

Discovering the "why" of your anger will provide a pathway of healing; that is, if you first ask the question and second do whatever it takes to heal and deal with the "why." You might have been asked this question by others throughout your life—Why are you so angry? And you likely couldn't give an answer that would satisfy. If your anger is justified, healing and forgiveness need to take place. If the source of your anger is due to lack of self-control and other awareness, you have some work to do to subdue your anger.

God asks such great questions in the first book of the Bible. In Genesis 3, after Adam and Eve ate the forbidden fruit, God asked them three questions that are used frequently in counseling. In verse 9, God asks, "Where are you?" Of course, God knew where they were, but he was asking them to surrender themselves—to reveal themselves. God then asks them in verse 10, "Who told you that you were naked?" Sometimes rage surfaces and others see what is hiding underneath the surface. The third question, in verse 13, was "What have you done?" The gravity of this question hits home for so many whose anger has produced consequences that many times cannot be reversed.

Perhaps your anger has caused you to question who's to blame, or to take the attitude that someone needs to pay. Instead of reacting, choose to reflect. Ask yourself these questions from the One who knows you best and loves you most. If you need another person to help you through this process, a trusted friend or counselor, take that step. God provides redemption and hope.

There was a long hard time when I kept far from me the remembrance of what I had thrown away when I was quite ignorant of its worth.

Charles Dickens

Make no excuses. Rationalize nothing. Blame no one. Humble yourself.

Beth Moore

If we will but let our God and Father work his will with us, there can be no limit to his enlargement of our existence.

George MacDonald

For Further Reflection

Psalm 119:5-6; Deuteronomy 6:5-6;
2 Corinthians 5:16–19

TODAY'S PRAYER

Father God, I want to enter into a new life, one that is reflective of you. Help me as I answer you, to be truthful, brave, and vulnerable, so that I can be the person you created me to be. Help me forgive, heal, and redeem my past and be more like you each day. Amen.

Day 12

Anger and Grief

He heals the brokenhearted and bandages their wounds.

Psalm 147:3

Grief is a universal experience. Yet each person will react and respond in his or her own way. You might have heard the concept that grief has stages that occur. Dr. Elizabeth Kubler-Ross, a psychiatrist, is credited with giving names to the stages in the grief process: denial, anger, bargaining, depression, and acceptance. Grief is caused by loss of any type, not just death. A person can experience loss in many ways and might not recognize how grief is affecting his or her life.

The anger stage occurs when you have to move on, and the loss you experienced is a stark contrast to the reality you had hoped for. You will experience frustration, irritation, and say things like "it's not fair," "God failed me," and "why me?" You might not realize you are becoming stuck in the anger stage, because your argument feels justified.

Sometimes the loss is so far removed from your anger that you might not connect the dots. You might not recognize that the anger you experience every day is tied to a loss in your past. You might be stuck in the anger stage as a defense to keep you from being vulnerable to experiencing loss ever again. Of course, that is impossible, because loss is a part of life.

What can you do if you recognize that your anger is anchored in grief? Attend to the loss through reading about grief, counseling, or a grief group. Recognizing that your anger might be a grief stage where you are stuck can allow healing to begin.

————————▶————————

I sat with my anger long enough until she told me her real name was grief.

Isaac Rowe

After a while, the anger I felt just sort of became part of me, like it was the only way I knew how to handle the grief. I didn't like who I'd become, but I was stuck in this horrible cycle of questions and blame.

Nicholas Sparks

Sharing our stories can also be a means of healing. Grief and loss may isolate us, and anger may alienate us. Shared with others, these emotions can be powerfully uniting, as we see that we are not alone, and realize that others weep with us.

Susan Wittig Albert

————————▶————————

For Further Reflection
2 Corinthians 4:17–18; Romans 8:26–28;
Revelation 21:4

TODAY'S PRAYER
Lord Jesus, my heart is broken with grief, and I am recognizing the damage it is causing in my life. I ask for your comfort and care as I offer to you this very painful wound. Thank you for your grace and mercy in my life. In your name I pray, Amen.

Changed Life

*Prove by the way you live that you have repented
of your sins and turned to God.*

MATTHEW 3:8

Most people enjoy hearing a "before and after" story, a compelling narrative where someone overcame seemingly insurmountable obstacles to experience victory. Movies and best-selling books are made of these storylines.

The "before" part of the narrative can be rough. Anger shows up in this part of the story almost every time. Of course, anger has many different ways of displaying itself: irritation, frustration, rage, isolation, bitterness, moodiness, and other not-so-obvious ways. For example, anger can hide in sadness, depression, and apathy. Anger can also hide in addiction, where a substance or habit is used to numb the anger.

When you start paying attention to the "before" in other people's stories, it might seem obvious where changes should be made—maybe some habits need adjusting, attitudes improved, or relationships restored. It seems so simple; why don't people just do the right thing?

Good question, and one you can ask yourself. What keeps you from doing what it takes to live the life God created for you?

Are you in the "before" or "after" part of your story? Are you living in a way that reveals the changed heart you have been given? Your salvation occurs the minute you accept Christ as your savior. Your life changes over time as you experience the love and grace given to you freely.

The Amplified Bible (AMP) Version of Matthew 3:8 says it this way: "So produce fruit that is consistent with repentance [demonstrating new behavior that proves a change of heart, and a conscious decision to turn away from sin]." As you discover where anger is still operating your life in the "before," surrender it to the Lord Jesus and begin to live freely in the "after"!

God's specialty is raising dead things to life and making impossible things possible. You don't have the need that exceeds his power.

Beth Moore

The remarkable part of Christianity is not that we have a Savior who came to deliver us but that we have a Savior who sees us for who we really are and loves us anyway.

Carey Nieuwhof

For Further Reflection
Jeremiah 24:7; Ezekiel 36:26; 2 Corinthians 7:10

TODAY'S PRAYER
Thank you, Jesus for my new life! May my life be a reflection of you. Help me to show grace and mercy as you have shown these to me. Help me to forgive and accept as you have done this for me. And as I live in your freedom, may it bring others to know you. Amen.

Be Free!

Therefore, since we are surrounded by such a huge crowd of witnesses to the life of faith, let us strip off every weight that slows us down, especially the sin that so easily trips us up. And let us run with endurance the race God has set before us.

HEBREWS 12:1

I s there ever a good use of anger? Of course. Anger is an internal alert system that warns us something is wrong. It can be a response to injustice or an alert to problems that need to be resolved. Anger becomes problematic when we become vigilant or aggressive about righting the wrong. However, when we can channel the energy that anger provides, we can make changes that benefit others. The challenge is to use the emotion for good, not get trapped by it.

Anger is a powerful force. If you have ever felt rage or been in an agitated state of frustration, you have felt the sense of release that occurs afterward. Some people actually use their anger as fuel to accomplish whatever task is in front of them. In sports, a mistake or a poor call by a referee can actually provide fuel for the best players to perform even better!

How is anger manifesting in your life? Do you feel like you are in competition with everyone and everything? Or are you able to channel this "alerting" anger to achieve positive change in your life? When something angers us, and we identify the wrong, we can take steps to make the differences needed in whatever the situation may be. Anger isn't an emotion to avoid or negate; instead, understand how it works and control it. As you encounter situations and people that arouse anger, don't let it trip you up.

To be angry is to revenge the faults of others on ourselves.

Alexander Pope

Each person who has changed the world for good in history are the ones who has managed to use their anger wisely.

Ozan Kulcu

Never underestimate anger's destructive power.

Billy Graham

For Further Reflection
Proverbs 16:32; Ephesians 4:26; Proverbs 25:28

TODAY'S PRAYER
Lord, you know how frustrating life can be! Help me to channel my anger to bring about good in the world. Help me to not give in to the emotional outburst, but rather submit to your will in all things. Help me to be free to accomplish the purpose you have for my life that it may bring glory to your name! Amen.

Day 15

Real Strength

This is my command—be strong and courageous!
Do not be afraid or discouraged. For the Lord
your God is with you wherever you go.

JOSHUA 1:9

Are you angry or are you afraid? Discerning between these two feelings can sometimes be difficult. These emotions feed into one another—fear arises when a threat is perceived (real or not), then anger kicks into action in defense and protection. Anger and fear often blend seamlessly, and that can prove a challenge when attempting to resolve these feelings.

Fear can be real or imagined, and some fears are legitimate concerns. For example, you might fear something happening to a loved one, which is a rational fear that most everyone experiences. If your loved one is threatened or hurt, your anger would rise to the threat. This is an example of healthy anger—you are having a reaction to the injustice or threat. But if your anger overwhelms you, it can create a bigger problem than first perceived.

The goal in addressing your anger isn't to numb it or to pretend to always be happy; the goal is learning to control the anger. All emotions require some level of control or we become governed by our feelings. Feelings and emotions are such a vital part of a healthy life. However, if one emotion starts to rule, it can cause difficulty in relationships, work, and our mental well-being.

When we experience fear, we can call upon God for courage and strength. God is with us, and remembering this truth can help us navigate our lives. When our anger is aroused, we can ask God to help us use it for good. Our courage and strength do not come from being angry; they come from abiding with God.

If one lets fear or hate or anger take possession of the mind, they become self-forged chains.

Helen Gahagan Douglas

Anger is the emotion we snatch up to avoid less comfortable feelings—confusion, fear, sadness.

Jill Herzig

You gain strength, courage and confidence by every experience in which you really stop to look fear in the face. You are able to say to yourself, 'I have lived through this horror. I can take the next thing that comes along.' You must do the thing you think you cannot do.

Eleanor Roosevelt

For Further Reflection

Psalm 118:5-6; Joshua 1:6-8; Proverbs 20:22

TODAY'S PRAYER

Dear God, thank you for your presence in my life. Help me to be aware that nothing I face is bigger than you. Give me wisdom and discernment to fight the battles you have for me and to know which to leave behind. Amen.

Day 16

When Anger Masks Fear

Fools vent their anger, but the wise quietly hold it back.

PROVERBS 29:11

Understanding anger can be confusing. It is not a sin to be angry, but in our anger, we are not to sin. We can express anger but not be vindictive or hateful in our anger. Today's scripture mentions the wisdom of holding back anger, yet we know that when we stuff our anger it can cause all kinds of issues. So, which is it? Vent or hold it back?

Obviously, the answer according to this scripture is to hold it back. But what does this look like? Does this mean you never express your anger? Of course not. Other versions of this same verse read:

- Fools give full vent to their rage, but the wise bring calm in the end. (NIV)

- Stupid people express their anger openly, but sensible people are patient and hold it back. (GNT)

- A rebel shouts in anger; a wise man holds his temper in and cools it. (TLB)

This makes it clear that the meaning is: when angry, use self-control. The degree to which you allow your anger to control you indicates whether you are a fool, stupid, or a rebel. Anger is a powerful emotion that can drive a person to say and do things they would never do when in their wise mind. The passion of anger has caused many regrets for people over the centuries and will continue to influence bad behavior as long as it is left unrestrained.

Have you experienced the full vent of your rage? Have you given in to expressing your anger in unhealthy ways? Begin today by pausing before you attack in anger. In this way, you become a wise person.

A man in a passion, rides a mad horse.

Benjamin Franklin

Anger is a valid emotion. It's only bad when it takes control and makes you do things you don't want to do.

Ellen Hopkins

Sometimes when I'm angry I have the right to be angry, but that doesn't give me the right to be cruel.

Bede Jarrett

For Further Reflection
Proverbs 19:19; James 1:26; Proverbs 14:16–17

TODAY'S PRAYER
Father God, help me to have a handle on my anger and emotions. Let me know your wisdom in dealing with things that are creating feelings of anger. Help me to be sensible and patient, not willing to be taken over by anger. For your glory, Amen.

Day 17

Let It Go

You have heard that our ancestors were told, 'You must not murder. If you commit murder, you are subject to judgment.' But I say, if you are even angry with someone, you are subject to judgment! If you call someone an idiot, you are in danger of being brought before the court. And if you curse someone, you are in danger of the fires of hell.

MATTHEW 5:21–22

Have you ever been so angry with someone that you uttered the phase "I could kill you"? You might have spent time thinking about how things would be so much better if the person you are furious with would just go away. Seems such a stretch that anyone would go as far as murder. The truth is that when we don't control our anger, our lives are in danger of being overtaken by it. Books, TV shows, and hit movies often incorporate plot lines centered on the consequences of uncontrolled anger.

You might be thinking you would never get to the point of murder, but untended anger plants the seeds of resentment and bitterness. Although you might never intend to harm another person, you must guard against murderous thoughts. Is there someone in your life right now whom you feel intense anger toward? If so, the path to freedom is forgiveness.

To forgive doesn't mean you forget; it means that you release yourself from the grip of the offense. Forgiveness is for you. When you are able to forgive, you are no longer fixated on making the person pay for what they have done, or focused on what you think they owe you. It isn't easy, but it is necessary—even required by God—that we forgive. Commit to clearing your heart and mind from whatever angered you. Begin the process of releasing yourself from the grips of what has threatened your life.

Forgiveness should start now. Putting off forgiving only deepens the wound. Clinging to bitterness postpones happiness. Life is short, time is fleeting. Today is the day to forgive.

Wilfred Peterson

Forgiveness is an act of the will, and the will can function regardless of the temperature of the heart.

Corrie ten Boom

Forgiveness liberates the soul. It removes fear. That is why it is such a powerful weapon.

Nelson Mandela

For Further Reflection

Proverbs 29:22; Galatians 5:19-26; Romans 12:21

TODAY'S PRAYER

Father God, forgive me for allowing my anger to rule my life. I pray that you will help me as I forgive those who have caused me pain. Provide comfort for me in place of my need for control, peace in place of my pain. Help me move forward in my life. May all of this be for your glory. Amen.

Day 18

Reactive Life

Short-tempered people do foolish things,
and schemers are hated.

PROVERBS 14:17

Are you easily angered? Does any minor infraction set you off? What do you do when service isn't what you expect, or someone makes a mistake, or what you hoped for doesn't happen? These things are part of life—for everyone. The world isn't out to get you, and things don't always go wrong for you, but such beliefs perpetuate the problem. If you recognize that frustrations and annoyances set you off disproportionately, you might be described as short-tempered. And likely the people around you feel like they walk on eggshells hoping not to feel your wrath.

Anger is a natural response to things that are wrong or that go wrong. But if everything is a trip wire to your landmine of fury, your anger is out of control. There are ways to handle the frustrations of life, and the first is to accept that not everything will go the way you planned or hoped. That isn't to say you must live in a state of defeat or pessimism. It means that when things go wrong, you need a way to deal with the strong feelings you experience.

Taking a breath before you react, counting to 10, and allowing some time and space before you respond are all ways to begin to control your reactivity. You don't have to attend every fight to which you are invited. Developing a peaceful nature takes time and deliberate focus. Learning how to respond in a healthy way to situations that anger you means uncovering and addressing the root issue that triggers your anger. By doing so, you will no longer be a ticking time bomb.

———————◢—————————

I came to realize that if people could make me angry, they could control me. Why should I give someone else such power over my life?

Dr. Ben Carson

When angry, count ten before you speak; if very angry, a hundred.

Thomas Jefferson

The one who cannot restrain their anger will wish undone, what their temper and irritation prompted them to do.

Horace

———————◢—————————

For Further Reflection

Proverbs 20:3; 2 Timothy 2:23-24;
1 Corinthians 13:4-5

TODAY'S PRAYER

Lord, when my quick reaction is less than what you desire from me, please help. Show me how to correct my responses and lead me to live in a way that reflects you. Forgive me for being unkind and rude and help me as I release my need to have everything work the way I think it needs to. I ask for your help in all of these things. Amen.

Bad Behavior

The wise are cautious and avoid danger;
fools plunge ahead with reckless confidence.

PROVERBS 14:16

"It's all fun and games until someone gets hurt." You may have heard this warning from a parent or teacher at some point in your life. Situations can get out of hand, especially if you have difficulty controlling your anger. Before you know it, your anger is controlling you and someone gets hurt.

Anger and rage can make bad conditions worse. A situation could begin with a heated discussion on a topic that two people have strong opinions about, and neither person can really hear what the other is saying. They might experience physical signs of tension such as clenched jaws, elevated heart rates, and raised voices. The amygdala, the part of the brain that is the warning system, causes people to react before the cortex, the part that provides judgment and thought, can provide a check. The argument might go too far and one person—or both—end up hurt, sometimes physically or spiritually but always emotionally.

There isn't a good excuse to go with the force of energy anger provides. We have to control our reactions and behavior. This maturing can begin in childhood with parents and adults who teach us how to manage our feelings and get along with others. However, even the best parenting cannot change a strong-willed person who is not amenable to learning to exert self-control.

Decide to exert your will to becoming wise. Then use your wisdom to work out differences and conflicts to bring about a redeeming resolution.

We must interpret a bad temper as a sign of inferiority.

Alfred Adler

People who fly into a rage always make a bad landing.

Will Rogers

There are some people who always seem angry and continuously look for conflict. Walk away; the battle they are fighting isn't with you, it is with themselves.

Anonymous

For Further Reflection

1 Peter 3:9; Ecclesiastes 7:9; Proverbs 15:18

TODAY'S PRAYER

Lord help me to be wise, to exert control over my anger, and use my voice for good. Strengthen my resolve to follow your will and not give in to my anger. I pray for discernment during important conversations so that they would be productive and not hurtful. In your name I pray, Amen.

Day 20

Love Is ...

Love is patient and kind. Love is not jealous or boastful or proud or rude. It does not demand its own way. It is not irritable, and it keeps no record of being wronged.

1 CORINTHIANS 13:4–5

God is love, and he loves us. The expression of God's love was to send his son, Jesus, to die for our sins on a cross. That is immeasurable love! The good news of God's love is that Jesus rose from the dead to give us eternal life.

The dark side of this redemption story is the suffering and anger Jesus endured. The beatings. The rage and hatred of the crowd as he carried that heavy cross down the streets. The crown of thorns pressed upon his head. On that cross, where he suffered taunts and torture from the soldiers, our sins were forgiven. Jesus who had no sin, who was peaceful and came to set us free, endured the violent anger of a sin-filled people, the very people he came to save.

If you have accepted Jesus as your savior, you have been saved from your sins and will spend eternity with God. You have the Holy Spirit to guide you in your life to be more like Jesus—loving, joyful, kind, peaceful, patient, self-controlled, gentle, and faithful. As you read these descriptions, consider whether you have these attributes. If not, the good news is that you can surrender to the Holy Spirit to develop this fruit in you! God provided a way for you to experience eternal life, and it begins now. That is how much God loves you!

But the man who is not afraid to admit everything that he sees to be wrong with himself, and yet recognizes that he may be the object of God's love precisely because of his shortcomings, can begin to be sincere. His sincerity is based on confidence, not in his own illusions about himself, but in the endless, unfailing mercy of God.

Thomas Merton

The sin underneath all our sins is to trust the lie of the serpent that we cannot trust the love and grace of Christ and must take matters into our own hands.

Martin Luther

Though our feelings come and go, God's love for us does not.

C.S. Lewis

For Further Reflection

John 3:16-17; Romans 8:38-39; Galatians 5:22-26

TODAY'S PRAYER

Thank you, God, for your love for me and the gift of eternal life! I pray that I will continue to be more like you and experience the freedom that you died to give me. Amen.

Day 21

Help Me Lord!

*Keep your servant from deliberate sins! Don't let them
control me. Then I will be free of guilt and innocent
of great sin. May the words of my mouth and the
meditation of my heart be pleasing to you,
O Lord, my rock and my redeemer.*

Psalm 19:13–14

Has anger become a habit in your life? That might seem like a strange question. Habits aren't feelings—or are they? Perhaps after a fit of anger you have offered the excuse, "I can't help it. It's just the way I am." Or maybe you say to yourself, "That is the last time I will lose my temper." Yet there is no change. Days become years and then a lifetime of being angry.

Ready to break this habit of anger? The first step is to recognize that anger is a habit and it has become your way of dealing with life. It can feel shameful to admit this habit, but you are loved by a forgiving God who wants to help you be the person you were created to be. Rather than making a public announcement that you are going to break this habit, keep your decision between you, God, and a couple of trustworthy people who will be supportive in your recovery.

Recovery from a habit or addiction requires a process of changing the way you think. Actually, everything will change. You will begin to experience life in a completely different way. The habit of anger will be broken and replaced with peace. Recovery doesn't mean you will never be angry again; anger has its place in our range of emotions. Breaking the habit means that you are no longer driven by the need to react in anger. The first step is to admit anger is a problem, so why not start today?

Bitterness: anger that forgot where it came from.

Alain de Botton

Holding anger is a poison.... It eats you from inside.... We think that by hating someone we hurt them.... But hatred is a curved blade ... and the harm we do to others ... we also do to ourselves.

Mitch Albom

If you want the great and mighty things God has for you, you must get to the root of your anger and deal with it.

Joyce Meyer

For Further Reflection

Ephesians 4:1-3; Colossians 1:3-8; Proverbs 22:24-25

TODAY'S PRAYER

Lord, I admit that anger has become a habit in my life that needs to be broken. Help me as I begin to make changes that will allow others to see you in me. Heal my brokenness and pain. Help me to receive your grace and mercy that you so freely offer. Thank you for hearing my prayer, Lord. Amen.

Day 22

Inside Out

And then he added, "It is what comes from inside that
defiles you. For from within, out of a person's heart,
come evil thoughts, sexual immorality, theft, murder,
adultery, greed, wickedness, deceit, lustful desires,
envy, slander, pride, and foolishness. All these vile
things come from within; they are what defile you."

MARK 7:20–23

Your thoughts and struggles—your inner life—will eventually show on the outside, in your attitude, behavior, and relationships. Does that surprise you? Scare you? Or do you think you can hide your struggles forever?

As with cancer that has to be removed before it infects the whole body, the things you hide in your heart will eventually take over. Your reactive anger might be caused by deep wounds in your heart that are not healed. Whatever pain, anger, or shame you don't deal with begins to alter the person you were created to be.

What comes to mind as you consider the condition of your heart? The things you carry inside can weigh you down, make life a burden, and begin to show on the outside in angry reactions, habits, and addictions. Jesus brings hope for a clean heart—healing from the inside out. Surrendering to God allows you to experience deep healing in the places inside that are causing shame, pain, and defensiveness. In Jesus you can experience the freedom of a transformed life!

Anger is a fuel. You need fuel to launch a rocket. But if all you have is fuel without any complex internal mechanism directing it, you don't have a rocket. You have a bomb.

Gil Schwartz

If anger isn't released, it "turns inward" and metamorphoses into another creature altogether.

Carol Tavris

Anger is poison. You must purge it from your mind or else it will corrupt your better nature.

Christopher Paolini

For Further Reflection

Ezekiel 36:25–27; Psalm 51:10; Proverbs 4:23

TODAY'S PRAYER

Lord Jesus, I offer you my heart and my inner life. Cleanse me of all that corrupts my life. Heal me of the wounds that are infected. I pray for your redeeming power to work in my life for your glory. Amen.

Settle Down

A gentle answer deflects anger,
but harsh words make tempers flare.

Proverbs 15:1

Are you able to discuss a topic you feel passionate about without losing your temper? If so, congratulations. But if you're reading this book, it's likely there are important conversations that never take place in your life because you cannot remain calm enough to engage effectively. You might become triggered by someone else's attitude, raised voice, or sarcastic response and grow louder and more emphatic, trying to communicate your strong feelings about the topic, because you don't feel heard by the other person.

Although you cannot control others, you can choose to control yourself. Recognize when the tension in a conversation begins, and take a breath. Maybe say, "Let's step back a second." Pay attention to your body's stress signals—an elevated heart rate or tension in your jaw or stomach. At this point, you can either give in to the sparks that are flying, or you can pause and show self-control by not fueling the argument. You can give yourself and the other person some space. You can say simply, "I need to think about this some more. Can we talk about it another time?" And say nothing more to escalate the conversation. Then offer some options to meet again on the topic.

You cannot go through life without having difficult conversations. You will experience unexpected upsets, because we live in relationship with other humans. We are all doing what we can, but it's not always our best. Recognize when anxiety or anger is driving a quick or harsh reaction in you. Controlling your reaction and working toward being responsive instead is the path toward healthy conversations, which can lead to positive changes.

Anger, in general, is healthy. Just like sadness or happiness, it's a normal emotion. Where people get into trouble is when anger becomes a behavior that is physically, verbally or emotionally inappropriate.

Carole D. Stovall

If you do not wish to be prone to anger, do not feed the habit; give it nothing which may tend to its increase.

Epictetus

Talk to people you disagree with, not about them.

Carey Nieuwhof

For Further Reflection

Philippians 4:8-9; 1 Timothy 1:5; Ephesians 2:10

TODAY'S PRAYER

Lord Jesus, I pray for the ability to have difficult conversations to bring about positive changes. I pray for your wisdom, grace, and strength to control my reactions. Help me to hear what I need to hear and not react in anger. Amen.

Day 24

Who's in Control?

Do not let sin control the way you live;
do not give in to sinful desires.

ROMANS 6:12

Anger management is an illusion of power; that is, it's your illusion that you can get your anger under wraps by "managing" the symptoms. It might seem like semantics, but the goal is to be able to control—not manage—your anger by treating it before the symptoms present. Control begins long before the feeling arises within you. Control is recognizing that the circumstances that lead you to "lose it" aren't the problem; your unresolved issues that inform your reaction to those circumstances are the problem.

You might have good reason to be angry. Perhaps you have been betrayed, experienced a great loss, or been treated horribly or unfairly. Maybe you have shame and guilt from sin in your life, and you try to stay "safe" behind the rage. Anger begins to surface when people are at their most vulnerable, and sometimes the anger is uglier than the original offense. Turning the focus on healing and resolving your internal struggles can enable you to use anger in a productive way.

Anger is not a sin, but in your anger, you can give in to sin. You can be swept away by the driving force and overreact, making poor decisions that can alter your life and relationships.

How can you take control of your anger? Begin by acknowledging that anger has controlled you long enough.

Release the root cause of your anger through prayer and counseling. Surrender to God the wrongs done to you. Grieve the losses and look for resolution and healing from the pain. Begin to recognize patterns of your anger; for example, perhaps when you are pressed for time or feel external stresses, anger flares easily. Be committed to finding healthy ways to control and express your anger.

As long as you live on earth, you won't see the end of injustices. Yet God desires for you to let go of injustices and hold on to His grace. Only He can give you the power to forgive those who have hurt you the deepest.

Paul Chappell

A Christian will find it cheaper to pardon than to resent. Forgiveness saves the expense of anger, the cost of hatred, the waste of spirits.

Hannah More

For Further Reflection

Proverbs 16:32; Nahum 1:3; Matthew 12:33–37

TODAY'S PRAYER

Lord, forgive my sin and help me to have control of the anger within and to resolve any wound, betrayal, fear, or threat. Help me to trust you to right the wrongs and to lead me in the way of understanding. Help me to use anger for good and not allow it to use me for evil. In your name I pray, Amen.

What's Your Problem?

The Lord replied, "Is it right for you to be angry about this?"

JONAH 4:4

The story of Jonah is about a man with a mission he didn't like who decided to do the opposite of what God asked. God told Jonah to preach repentance to the people of Ninevah, but Jonah disagreed with that plan. He didn't want the Ninevites to repent and experience God's mercy. He wanted God to punish them for their wickedness. In fact, he went to such extremes to avoid obeying God that God provided the ultimate "time out"—three days in the belly of a fish.

When that fish vomited Jonah onto land, he finally submitted to God's plan and preached to the Ninevites. The people of Ninevah repented of their sins, experienced revival, and ended their evil ways. However, Jonah's anger remained.

Have you ever disagreed with God? Have you tried to ignore what God has been asking you to do because you didn't want others to receive the grace and forgiveness you have received from God? Our anger and defiance hurts us and can get us off track with the plans God has for our lives.

Are you angry with God?

Maybe you don't disagree with God's calling as Jonah did, but maybe you're frustrated within your calling. Maybe you're angry about injustice in the world or a series of failures in your life. Know that God can handle your anger and invites you to share it as part of your communication with him. When you are disappointed or upset with God, don't let those emotions drive you from your heavenly Father. Instead, talk with him through prayer or journaling. Then listen for the still, small voice that will provide a path of healing and comfort.

Most people who are angry with God are angry with him for being God. They're not angry because he has failed to deliver what he promised. They're angry because he has failed to deliver what they have craved, expected or demanded.

Paul David Tripp

Forgive God if you are angry with Him because your life didn't turn out the way you thought it should. God is always just. There may be things you don't understand, but God loves you, and people make a serious mistake when they don't receive help from the only One who can truly help them.

Joyce Meyer

For Further Resources:

Psalm 9:10; Proverbs 19:3; Isaiah 46:3-5, 9

TODAY'S PRAYER

Father God, you are my creator and Lord. When my anger is directed toward you, help me to submit to your will, knowing it is the best plan for my life. May I trust you and be secure in my relationship with you to share my frustrations and hurts, knowing you hear and will meet my needs. In your name, Amen.

Day 26

You Blew It

Have mercy on me, O God, because of your unfailing love.
Because of your great compassion, blot out the stain of my sins.

Psalm 51:1

You blew it. You went too far and now it feels like all is lost. Sometimes the consequences of behavior cause irreparable damage. When you go into a rage and your anger creates pain and division, the situation might feel beyond hope. Sometimes connections do break down. Someone you have a relationship with might find your anger too much to continue to take on, and they choose to set a boundary or leave the relationship. Anger begins as a feeling and then becomes behavior, which, if not controlled, wreaks havoc in your life.

The good news is redemption is available. You can ask God to forgive you and begin to heal so that anger no longer controls your life. You can take steps to ask forgiveness from those you have hurt. You can make amends for the results of your behavior. The other person is not obligated to forgive you, or stay in the relationship, but you do what you can and then let it rest. The work is yours; the other person is not required to respond in a certain way. It's wonderful if the relationship is restored, but sometimes that is not possible. Regardless of the outcome, you still have to work on controlling your anger.

Even if you ask and receive forgiveness from the people you hurt, you might still have residual guilt and shame, which if not dealt with has the power to become anger all over again.

The goal is to completely deal with whatever seeks to control you. Gaining freedom from anger is a daily process of asking God to clean your heart and provide guidance for each day. As the Holy Spirit guides your life, you will grow in self-control rather than anger.

Getting over a painful experience is much like crossing monkey bars. You have to let go at some point in order to move forward.

C.S. Lewis

Forgiveness is the economy of the heart. Forgiveness saves the expense of anger, the cost of hatred, the waste of spirits.

Hannah More

The voice of sin is loud, but the voice of forgiveness is louder.

Dwight L. Moody

For Further Reflection
Isaiah 1:18; Micah 7:18-19; 1 John 1:9

TODAY'S PRAYER

Lord God, my sin of anger is great and wants to control my life. I ask for your redeeming power to clean my heart, mind, and soul. I pray for those who have been hurt by my anger to receive healing and comfort from you, and if possible, that they would be able to forgive me for their peace of mind. Thank you for your grace and mercy. Amen.

And Then ... People

*Do not seek revenge or bear a grudge against a fellow
Israelite, but love your neighbor as yourself. I am the Lord.*

LEVITICUS 19:18

Have you ever had a day where you woke up feeling refreshed, got ready for the day without any problems, and had a plan for how the day would go? And then ... people. Sometimes you might feel that certain people exist to wreck your life, cause you inconvenience, and in general irritate you. Even though you might not lose your temper, anger starts to simmer below the surface, bubbling and threatening to boil over at any minute.

This is not the way to go through life, especially as a believer and follower of Jesus. It's not the way of freedom. Yes, you will have frustrations, irritations, and mishaps. And getting upset about those things is understandable, especially when they make your day difficult. It would be just as bad to be numb to the struggles of life or act fake-happy when situations are difficult. But you have to learn how to deal with the things of life and the people you encounter in a healthy and loving way.

Holding a grudge or a negative attitude toward people can quickly shift to anger. As you recognize what is bubbling underneath, surrender that emotion—and those difficult situations you're facing—to God and move into freedom. This will equip you to handle whatever difficulties or minor irritations come your way. You will be more like the One who created you!

If I belittle those whom I am called to serve, talk of their weak points in contrast perhaps with what I think of as my strong points; if I adopt a superior attitude, forgetting "Who made thee to differ? and what hast thou that thou hast not received?" then I know nothing of Calvary love.

Amy Carmichael

We choose what attitudes we have right now. And it's a continuing choice.

John C. Maxwell

Words can never adequately convey the incredible impact of our attitudes toward life. The longer I live the more convinced I become that life is 10 percent what happens to us and 90 percent how we respond to it.

Chuck Swindoll

For Further Reflection

Psalm 34:17; Hebrews 4:14-16; Jeremiah 17:9-10

TODAY'S PRAYER

Lord Jesus, thank you for all you have so graciously done for me. May my attitude reflect you, with patience, wisdom, compassion, and grace. Help me to redirect myself when frustrations start to distance me from who you created me to be. Amen.

Parental Anger

Fathers, do not provoke your children to anger by the way you treat them. Rather, bring them up with the discipline and instruction that comes from the Lord.

EPHESIANS 6:4

What do you do when as a parent you're about to lose your cool? Maybe you've told the children something multiple times and yet get no cooperation. Parents often experience anger in raising children, but unfortunately, it isn't always handled correctly.

As a child, you might have been on the receiving end of a parent's anger, or you might be struggling with anger as you parent now. If you recognize that you are struggling with reactions that are too harsh, and perhaps are reminiscent of your childhood, you can get help. Maybe you don't know how to deal with the anger that rises when children are disobedient. Recognize the patterns in your parenting, and notice what happens when anger begins to build. What physical symptoms do you recognize before the outburst? Learn to recognize your anger is building and take a minute to calm down before addressing the issue. You might ask for help from your spouse or another trusted person.

Are you overwhelmed? Perhaps you are feeling guilt or shame over how you treated your children when you had a short fuse. The same guilt and shame can actually prevent the cycle from being broken. If your reaction was out of line with how you want to parent, recognize that. Apologize to your children for your behavior. This doesn't absolve the disobedience; rather, it sets the tone for the relationship. Address what needs to be corrected but without the drama.

You might need to do some deeper work if you had a harsh parent or have been a harsh parent. Meet with a counselor to work through forgiving your parent(s) for the harm they caused you. Begin to make changes in your own parenting.

It is better to bind your children to you by a feeling of respect and by gentleness than by fear.

Terence

Don't worry that children never listen to you; worry that they are always watching you.

Robert Fulghum

For Further Reflection

Proverbs 22:6; 2 Corinthians 4:16–18; Psalm 139:23–24

TODAY'S PRAYER

Father God, help me be the parent you have called me to be, leading my children to follow you. Forgive me where I have failed and help my children forgive me and live their life without the pain of my failings. I pray that I can forgive any grievances I might be holding onto from my own childhood so that I may live free of the past. Amen.

Slow to Anger

The Lord is compassionate and merciful, slow to get angry and filled with unfailing love. He will not constantly accuse us, nor remain angry forever.

PSALM 103:8–9

Some of us are fearful of the anger of God. Maybe we have read stories in the Bible where it is obvious that God was angry against sin and sent judgment against it—Sodom and Gomorrah, Uzziah and the Ark of the Covenant, and the great Flood—just to name a few. Some of us live under a fear of God's anger, afraid he will strike us down at any slight error or sin. Sometimes we lose sight of the fact that God is angry about the sin but loves the sinner. He is focused on redeeming our lives—not destroying us.

The Psalmist tells us that God is "compassionate and merciful." He is not hot tempered but "slow to get angry" and "filled with unfailing love." Does that sound like you? The next verse says, "He will not constantly accuse us, nor remain angry forever." Does that sound like you? Unfortunately, the reality for many of us is that we are impatient, unforgiving, quick tempered, unfaithful, grudge holding, and resentful. That is not who God is, and he desires that we would be more like him.

How do you get to this place in your development? The Holy Spirit working in you can help you overcome the control anger has on you. Start today by forgiving someone who has hurt you. Make one good decision, followed by other good decisions (not bringing up the offense, letting go of the resentment, etc.). Make room for other people's mistakes, trying to work things out rather than cut them off. Take the first steps, and as you continue to work on becoming the person God created you to be, you will grow in the attributes listed in Psalm 103:8-9. It's a worthy calling!

Look for yourself, and you will find in the long run only hatred, loneliness, despair, rage, ruin, and decay. But look for Christ and you will find him, and with him everything else thrown in.

C.S. Lewis

Jesus did invite people to follow him into that sort of life from which behavior such as loving one's enemies will seem like the only sensible and happy thing to do. For a person living that life, the hard thing to do would be to hate the enemy, to turn the supplicant away, or to curse the curser…. True Christlikeness, true companionship with Christ, comes at the point where it is hard not to respond as he would.

Dallas Willard

For Further Reflection

Ephesians 4:22-24; Titus 3:1-2; Philippians 1:6

TODAY'S PRAYER

Lord, I want to be more like you. Your lovingkindness is better than I deserve! Help me to offer to others the love and mercy you freely give to me. May my character be more like yours with every day of my life. I ask for your help. Amen.

Day 30

Course Correction

Three different times I [Paul] begged the Lord to take
it away. Each time he said, "My grace is all you need.
My power works best in weakness." So now I am
glad to boast about my weaknesses, so that
the power of Christ can work through me.

2 CORINTHIANS 12:8–9

When you think back on things that you prayed for and didn't receive, what is your response? Maybe you are thinking of painful losses—how you prayed earnestly for a different outcome, and you don't understand why it happened. Tragic loss, betrayal and many other challenges are part of living in a fallen world, and yet God can use these things for good. Your anger toward God for these types of losses and challenges is part of processing grief. You can go to the Lord with your pain and frustration, and he wants you to. The bitterness and resentment that threaten your relationship with God would be another loss that could be devastating. Express your anger and confusion to God. Work it out so that you aren't lost too.

What about the anger you have toward God when things don't go your way in other circumstances? Perhaps you were hoping for a raise, or maybe you were passed over for a promotion or recognition. Maybe you feel like you are running up against a wall and God isn't there to help you. Or maybe you are praying for something that really isn't what God has planned for you.

You can't always get what you want, and that can be a really good thing, but not if you expect God to be like Santa. If that is your version of the Most High God, you are going to be disappointed and likely be frustrated with life and God. His training, standard, and desire for your life have a definitive path to make you more like Christ. The decision will be yours; will you accept course correction when it occurs, or will you refuse God and become angry and disconnected?

———————

Could it be that God is so intensely personal that he would burn down your world in hopes of building it back?

Matt Chandler

I have not lost faith in God. I have moments of anger and protest. Sometimes I have been closer to him for that reason.

Elie Wiesel

———————

For Further Reflection

Romans 8:26–28; Lamentations 3:55–57; 1 Peter 5:6–7

TODAY'S PRAYER

Lord, I don't understand why things happen the way they do. Help me to trust you and let go of any resentment that may keep me from experiencing all you have for me—even when it looks different than my expectations. I desire your will for my life. Amen.

Day 31

Enemy Love

You have heard the law that says, "Love your neighbor"
and hate your enemy. But I say, love your enemies!
Pray for those who persecute you!

MATTHEW 5:43–44

Many times, anger is driven by broken relationships. We might think of people who have broken trust or wounded us to be our enemies. We feel justified in our anger toward them. We think that if other people heard what happened to us, they would understand our anger and probably take our side.

Well, Jesus has another approach—to love our enemies. It's hard to even imagine what that means when we have so much anger toward those who have caused tremendous pain in our lives. What does it mean to love them?

It starts with another teaching of Jesus: forgiveness. To love our enemies means to forgive them. Forgiveness releases them of any obligation to us. It doesn't make the wrong right; rather, it frees us from the wrong. Sometimes people mistakenly think forgiveness means we are OK with the offense. This isn't true. Forgiveness doesn't correct the offense; it begins the healing process for us.

Another part of loving our enemies is praying for them. This act is probably even more difficult to comprehend than forgiving them. Jesus teaches us to love our enemies because doing so heals our hearts. Loving our enemies doesn't mean we will be in a relationship with them. That is dependent on their work of restitution with us. If reconciliation happens, that is wonderful. But many times it doesn't.

As long as we nurture our offense, our anger takes root in our hearts and begins to affect everything in our lives. By loving our enemies, we free ourselves from the past. The process of forgiveness and healing is not quick and easy, but it is the way Jesus taught us to live our lives, and it's the best way.

Forgiveness is above all a personal choice, a decision of the heart to go against natural instinct to pay back evil with evil.

Pope John Paul II

Forgiveness does not mean ignoring what has been done or putting a false label on an evil act. It means, rather, that the evil act no longer remains as a barrier to the relationship. Forgiveness is a catalyst creating the atmosphere necessary for a fresh start and a new beginning.

Dr. Martin Luther King Jr.

For Further Reflection

Proverbs 24:17; Luke 6:35; Proverbs 25:21

TODAY'S PRAYER

Lord Jesus, help me forgive those who have hurt me. Heal my wounds and allow me to live in freedom. Thank you for loving me and for helping me as I love my enemies. Amen.

Day 32

Family Affair

Then Jacob became furious with Rachel. "Am I God?" he asked.

Genesis 30:2

The Bible is full of accounts of men and women who desired to follow God's plan for their life and encountered obstacles. The story of Jacob is one such story. Not only did he lie to steal his father's blessing from his brother, but then when he sets out to start his family, he gets taken advantage of by his father-in-law. Then his wives (who are sisters) begin to compete with each other, and he is frustrated.

Anger directly connects to the lack of control people feel they have over circumstances. God is in control; you are not. You have to accept this truth in your struggle with anger. When frustrating situations come your way, you might feel angry and want to express that anger to anyone in the vicinity. The need to vent is understandable. But family members are the people in the closest proximity, and they are the ones who experience the brunt of the anger.

In the situation with Jacob and Rachel, Jacob was furious. But as you read the whole story, you'll see that literally everyone in the family takes turns being angry—Jacob, his father Isaac, and his brother Esau ... and then that anger carries into the next generation to Jacob's sons.

Is there ongoing anger in your family? Maybe it's not the shouting-at-each-other type of anger. It might be bitterness that seethes and is tearing at the fabric of your relationship.

Examine where anger might be affecting your family. Decide to change the way you express your anger. Instead of attacking the person, take a breath, state that you are upset, and then talk through the issue. Or decide to come back at a time when you are calmer to discuss it. Handling your anger in a healthy way could set a new path for the whole family.

Deep inside us, we know what every family therapist knows: the problems between the parents become the problems within the children.

Roger Gould

Family quarrels are bitter things. They don't go according to any rules. They're not like aches or wounds, they're more like splits in the skin that won't heal because there's not enough material.

F. Scott Fitzgerald

All happy families resemble one another, but each unhappy family is unhappy in its own way.

Leo Tolstoy

For Further Reflection

1 John 4:20; Proverbs 11:29; Psalm 133

TODAY'S PRAYER

Father God, Thank you for my family. Help me recognize when I am not loving or not controlling my reactions. Help me offer grace with truth and seek to connect, where possible, with my family. In your name, Amen.

Day 33

Step by Step

*Rejoice in our confident hope. Be patient
in trouble and keep on praying.*

ROMANS 12:12

G od has a calling for each of us, yet our journeys
will not always be easy. There will be times when
one extreme emotion or another will try to get us
off our path. The fury of frustration and blood-boiling rage
may threaten to overwhelm and bring us down a road that
is a dead end, spiritually and relationally. What can we do
when the strong pull of anger threatens to redirect our steps?

Take it one step at a time. By breaking things down, the
all-encompassing turbulence of rage becomes manageable.
Concentrate solely on the step at hand, be mindful, and trust
God to lead you forward.

These steps will give you a solid plan to turn to when
emotions rise too high:

Step 1: Rejoice in the confident hope of Christ. He has
promised to never leave us or forsake us (Deut. 31:6), to
be our ever-present help in times of trouble (Psalm 46:1).
Focusing on these positive truths will help you to push
out the negativity of anger.

Step 2: Be patient in trouble. This may seem impossible
against the fuel of anger, but remember to let the hope of
Christ strengthen you. Through Jesus, your patience can grow
and be used as an opposing force to the reactions of anger.

Step 3: Keep on praying! We must never forget the power of prayer to help us deal with the challenges and difficulties of our daily life.

We can depend on God to direct our path. He is more powerful than any emotion. When things threaten our walk, we are able—with Almighty God—to stay the course, step by step.

A man who walks with God always gets to his destination.

Henrietta C. Mears

There is nothing God doesn't know about your life. You may know the past and present, but God also knows the future. Choose today to walk securely - not in what you know, but in what you believe.

Dr. David Jeremiah

God has a program of character development for each of us. He wants others to look at our lives and say, He walks with God, for he lives like Christ.

Erwin W. Lutzer

For Further Reflection
Psalm 119:133; Psalm 37:7; Jeremiah 29:11

TODAY'S PRAYER
Lord Jesus, thank you for your abiding love, endless hope, and graceful direction for my life. When the things of this world threaten my walk, I humbly ask for your help as I walk in your ways that I may live a life worthy of your calling. In your name, Amen.

Self-Control

Stay alert! Watch out for your great enemy, the devil. He prowls around like a roaring lion, looking for someone to devour.

1 Peter 5:8

Have you ever been so angry that you felt out of control? Your heart starts beating fast, your breathing becomes shallow, and you're about to blow your top. Everyone has these moments, and they seem to come unannounced, unplanned, and definitely unwanted.

If you want to work toward controlling your anger, you have to decide to do so, and you have to *decide* long before you find yourself in a situation that triggers those emotions. Maybe you've decided to never raise your voice in anger. You might not be 100% successful the next time your anger resurfaces, but work at decreasing your volume, and eventually those efforts will make a difference. Pray and ask God to help you with the steps you're taking.

If you have already let your anger fly and need to apologize, do so. Even if time has passed, making amends for losing your temper can begin a new path for your future. You cannot move forward with the decision to control your anger without repairing whatever damage your anger has done. Humility is a part of controlling your anger, and owning your part and making things right is part of humility.

Finally, recognize what is pushing your buttons and begin to work on the buttons themselves.

As you stay alert to your warning signs of anger, you develop self-control—and have the opportunity to change the future.

———————▸———————

I want my life to radiate what happens when God has a person's heart at his full control, when every event or circumstance is simply another avenue to know him better and show forth his glory.

Priscilla Shirer

I am a spiritual being…. After this body is dead, my spirit will soar. I refuse to let what will rot rule the eternal. I choose self-control. I will be drunk only by joy. I will be impassioned only by my faith. I will be influenced only by God. I will be taught only by Christ.

Max Lucado

Anger is not in itself sinful, but…it may be the occasion for sin. The issue of self-control is the question of how we deal with anger. Violence, tantrums, bitterness, resentment, hostility, and even withdrawn silence are all sinful responses to anger.

R. C. Sproul

———————▸———————

For Further Reflections

James 1:19-20; Ephesians 4:14-15; Hebrews 12:14-15

TODAY'S PRAYER

Lord, I am making the decision to control my anger. Help me to recognize when I am struggling to keep it under control, and please provide a way out. Help me to make amends to those I have hurt with my anger. I want to be self-controlled and live a life that reflects you. Amen.

Day 35

Blinded by Anger

See that no one pays back evil for evil, but always
try to do good to each other and to all people.

1 THESSALONIANS 5:15

We don't always see things the way they are. We see our perspective, which is valid, but it might not be the whole story. It is difficult to see another person's viewpoint, especially when anger blinds us. We become committed to our version of the situation.

The anger might be justified; a terrible offense was done and it's nearly impossible to let it go from our minds. We try to make sense of it. Maybe we've even tried to consider the other side of the story. But this terrible thing—this wrong that cannot be undone—should never have happened. It calls for retaliation. It must be made right. How can there be any other way to see it?

We need a new viewpoint, a shift in perspective. God provides mercy and grace to bring healing to our lives. God offers peace so that the reverberation of the wrong doesn't continue to claim power over our lives.

As you read this and think about the unthinkable wrong that has happened, take a minute to offer the wound to God for healing. Trust him to right the wrong—in his time and way— and know that as you let go of the justified anger, you will regain your life. It will look a bit different, but in a good way. The grieving process will give way to rebuilding something new. Something refined by grace and mercy and forgiveness.

Being blinded by anger restricts your view of blessings God has for you. Allow God to handle the grievance and receive from him the peace that passes all understanding. It's time for a clearer view!

It's time to let God's love cover all things in your life. All secrets. All hurts. All hours of evil, minutes of worry.

Max Lucado

When you are troubled and worried and sick at heart/ And your plans are upset and your world falls apart,/ Remember God's ready and waiting to share/ The burden you find much too heavy to bear–/ So with faith, "Let Go and Let God" lead your way/ Into a brighter and less troubled day.

Helen Steiner Rice

Some people believe holding on and hanging in there are signs of great strength. However, there are times when it takes much more strength to know when to let go and then do it.

Ann Landers

For Further Reflections

Philippians 3:13-14; Isaiah 43:18-19; Psalm 46:10-11

TODAY'S PRAYER

Lord, you know I am so very angry about the wrong that has happened. It has become my battle to win, and yet I know there is no victory in that battle. I surrender to you my anger; heal me and help me move forward in your peace. Amen.

Day 36

It's All Too Much!

*Moses heard all the families standing in the doorways
of their tents whining, and the Lord became extremely
angry. Moses was also very aggravated.... "I can't carry
all these people by myself! The load is far too heavy!"*

Numbers 11:10, 14

As the leader of the nation of Israel during its journey from slavery in Egypt to the land God had promised, Moses keenly felt the pressure and weight of his responsibilities before God and the people. As the children of Israel faced repeated challenges and trials during their wilderness trek, Moses struggled with how to handle their constant complaining, stubbornness, and disobedience. At times he felt exasperated and overwhelmed.

Have you ever felt your anger rising due to the pressure you are experiencing? You might not be leading a whole nation to freedom as Moses was, but you're not exempt from the stress of life, which can get overwhelming. Sometimes the pressure is too much, and you explode. When that happens, the pressure releases but the problem remains. You have to step back and rethink your approach.

Moses had to reassess his circumstances frequently over the forty-year journey. In Numbers 11, he cried out to God, "I can't carry all these people by myself! The load is far too heavy!" In the rest of this account, Moses expressed his heart to God. He was truly overwhelmed and wanted to be done with it all. God heard his cries, provided for the

Israelites repeatedly, and brought them into the promised land. Deuteronomy 29:5 says, "For forty years, I led you through the wilderness, yet your clothes and sandals did not wear out."

God's faithfulness can help you carry whatever pressure you are under. Ask God for help. Share with him the struggle you are feeling. No matter where the pressure is coming from, God can provide. When you feel like it's all too much, go to the One who will provide.

For every door God opens, there will be something in front of it to test you.

T. D. Jakes

May God remind us daily—no matter what kind of obstacles we face—that we are loved and empowered by the One who brought the universe into existence with the mere sound of his voice. Nothing is impossible for him.

Beth Moore

For Further Reflection
Ephesians 3:20-21; Philippians 3:12-14; Psalm 33:20-22

TODAY'S PRAYER
Jesus, I am overwhelmed, and my reactions are not honorable. Please help me trust you with my frustrations and pressure. I know you have a plan, and I am willing to do whatever it takes to fulfill your purpose in my life. Thank you for your provision and grace. Amen.

Day 37

Watch Your Words

His wife said to him, "Are you still trying to maintain your integrity? Curse God and die."

JOB 2:9

Have you said things in anger that you regret afterwards? You're not alone. After Job suffered a period of cataclysmic destruction and loss, his wife was angry, hurt, and probably scared. It was at this point she advised: "Curse God and die."

When we are angry and frustrated, we are likely to say things that are very damaging to the other person. Maybe we really don't mean what we say. Maybe we do. But words are powerful, and when we are angry, we lose control of our filter and our ability to hold our tongue. Unfortunately, it is hard to "unhear" what is said in anger.

If losing control of your words in anger has been your pattern, remember that the frustration doesn't appear at the moment you are spewing words. It is below the surface, sometimes buried deep within. Past wounds and relational struggles have been tucked inside and never dealt with; at the point of frustration, the words and the anger come flying out.

Life is really hard at times, and the need to express pain, frustration, and rage are part of dealing with the difficulty. When you sense feelings of anger, try to acknowledge the other feelings that accompany it. For example, "I feel frustrated because the line is taking so long and there should be a better way to do this." Or, "I can't believe this happened, and I am so sad and unsure of what will happen next." Both types of situations can prompt words and reactions that make things worse. Identifying underlying emotions and stressors can help you process what you're experiencing and work to behave in a way that leads to a more productive outcome.

Journaling, praying, and talking with trusted friends and family on a regular basis can help process your feelings, relieve the build-up of emotion, and provide insight into how to deal with the challenges.

———————————

Anger is the feeling that makes your mouth work faster than your mind.

Evan Esar

A slip of the foot you may soon recover, but a slip of the tongue you may never get over.

Benjamin Franklin

———————————

For Further Reflection

Proverbs 18:21; Colossians 4:6; Matthew 15:18

TODAY'S PRAYER

Father, help me remember the power of my words. Help me to recognize when things bother me and to bring them to you and others who can help me. Help me keep short accounts so I don't carry the burden. Thank you for helping me. Amen.

Day 38

Patience is a Virtue

*A fool is quick-tempered, but a wise person
stays calm when insulted.*

PROVERBS 12:16

I f you have been dealing with anger issues, you likely
have an issue with impatience. The two go together, and
sometimes impatience looks like anger and vice versa.

For example, we all have days when we don't feel like we
have enough time. The truth is, we have too much to do in
the time allotted, and we haven't accepted this reality. We
don't like to admit limitations and often try to push ourselves
beyond our ability. Time is fixed, and we have to manage it.
If we recognize that we are irritable or angry because of a
lack of time, we must make space in our schedule and say no
to things we can't do. This decision can be difficult, because
it bumps up against our belief that we can do whatever we
want, whenever we want.

The other place where impatience leads to anger is in our
relationships. When we don't recognize that people are who
they are, and that they might not be able—or want—to make
choices we think are best, we might feel frustrated. Maybe
someone we care about has an addiction, and we have given
them multiple opportunities to course-correct. Or maybe
we want someone to do more with their life because we
think it reflects on our worth. Control and co-dependency
lie at the core of this type of impatience. We must address
those issues, realizing that even though we might have good

intentions or think we know what's best for someone else, we cannot control others.

Being patient isn't a one-time decision; patience is a resource you must continually stock up on. If impatience is driving you to anger, create space in your life to experience more peace even when things don't go the way you want.

Impatience can cause wise people to do foolish things.

Janette Oke

Those speak foolishly who ascribe their anger or their impatience to such as offend them or to tribulation. Tribulation does not make people impatient but proves that they are impatient. So, everyone may learn from tribulation how his heart is constituted.

Martin Luther

For Further Reflections
Psalm 37:7–9; 1 Thessalonians 5:14; Romans 5:3–4

TODAY'S PRAYER
Lord, help me increase my patience. Help me understand and discern what is for me to do and not to do. I pray for your strength and insight as I search for the areas that are pushing my limits and bringing out the worst in me. I want to be more like you each day. Amen.

Day 39

No One is Perfect

For everyone has sinned; we all fall short
of God's glorious standard.

ROMANS 3:23

One of the driving forces in anger is disappointment, and disappointment in people and their behavior is a big part of that force. Expecting that people should do things the way you think they should brings frustration. If you have repeated frustrating experiences with certain people (family, spouse, neighbors, coworkers) it is sure to bring out the worst in you.

If anger has become characteristic in your life and you generally blame this anger on others, it's likely not the other people who have the problem. Someone might ask, "Why are you so angry?" or "Why are you so irritated?" and you might answer, "I'm not." You might be unaware that your anger has surfaced. You might have a version of yourself in your own mind that doesn't match the truth.

If you are often focused on how other people make you angry or can't do anything right, it's time for a self-check. No one is perfect. Not you, not anyone. When you can fully accept this, you will begin to experience less anger and frustration. As your perspective changes, your expectations will change, and you will find yourself with more patience. When you realize everyone has areas they struggle with, you can become more tolerant and kind. You will be less likely to judge others, show contempt, or lash out when situations don't go as planned.

Try seeing yourself from another perspective. Have a conversation with a trusted friend or family member and ask them how they experience your anger. If you start feeling defensive, remember the goal is to just listen. You can control your anger through awareness, acceptance, and acknowledgment that no one is perfect!

Anger shows contempt. Anger tears down. It kills relationships.

Ed Welch

You can't change what you don't acknowledge.

Phil McGraw

Every day we have plenty of opportunities to get angry, stressed or offended. But what you're doing when you indulge these negative emotions is giving something outside yourself power over your happiness. You can choose to not let little things upset you.

Joel Osteen

For Further Reflections

Ephesians 4:32; Matthew 7:1-2; Colossians 3:12

TODAY'S PRAYER

Lord Jesus, remind me of how much you have done for me. Help me to be kind and patient in all of my relationships, whether close or casual, that my character would reflect you. Amen.

Day 40

Servant Attitude

A servant of the Lord must not quarrel but must be kind to everyone, be able to teach, and be patient with difficult people.

2 Timothy 2:24

If we are followers of Christ, we are in a lifelong process of being transformed so that our behavior and attitude becomes more Christ-like. We will have areas to work on as long as we are alive. And if that makes you mad, well, that's something else to work on!

What does it mean to have a servant attitude? Does it mean that you let everyone have their way or never disagree with anyone? Not really. It means that you have control of your emotions, attitude, and intentions. It means that you are aware and mindful of the needs around you and do what you can to help others.

A servant attitude also means that you recognize your own needs and tend to them. When you have addressed your needs, you are able to give from what you have. If you feel angry when someone asks for help or you resent having to help someone, you likely have some deficits in your need tank. Are you hungry, angry, lonely, or tired? This HALT acronym can help you identify when your attitude may need adjusting. Sometimes we can become angry when our blood sugar dips, hormones change, or are in need of sleep. We are physical, emotional, spiritual, and mental beings with many different aspects that need attention.

When we realize all that God has for our lives, we will also be able to discern attitudes that hamper our ability to live selflessly and lovingly with those around us. To be angry or irritable with people won't help us reach many for the kingdom. However, with a loving attitude and changed heart, we will make a difference in the world!

To lose yourself in righteous service to others can lift your sights and get your mind off personal problems, or at least put them in proper focus.

Ezra Taft Benson

Always have a willing hand to help someone, you might be the only one that does.

Roy T. Bennett

There is no exercise better for the heart than reaching down and lifting people up.

John Holmes

For Further Reflection

Philippians 2:3-5; Isaiah 43:18-19; Matthew 15:11

TODAY'S PRAYER

Lord Jesus, thank you for changing my life! May that change be obvious to others as I become more like you and serve others. May your kingdom come, and your will be done in my life. Amen.

The Right Fight

Don't pick a fight without reason,
when no one has done you harm.

PROVERBS 3:30

There's an old saying, "You don't have to go to every fight you are invited to." Over your lifetime, you will be invited to plenty! Disagreements and fights are unavoidable. But how you manage them will make all the difference.

You might be someone who is more of a fighter, someone who identifies the wrong immediately and needs to make it right. When a fight stays focused on making things better or correcting injustice, that's good. But keep in mind that being "right" is a perspective, and yours might not be right. This is why conversations break down and relationships sometimes fail—we cannot always see the other person's viewpoint.

If you are always determined to be right, you will find yourself in more fights than other people do. Sometimes you might not realize that your stubbornness is actually the problem, that you have a strong need to be right. Ask yourself a few questions: Do I have to have the last word in a discussion? Do I feel unheard in heated discussions, like I have to explain again or give the "facts" another way? Do I tend to rehash the conversation later with a friend or loved one to verify I'm "really" right?

If this sounds like you, it's time to fight the need-to-be-right fight. And if you recognize that your need to be right might be connected to a root of anger, begin to work on discernment as well as your approach. Many situations in life will need your "fight" for the right cause or outcome. But be wise! Work hard not to get drawn into the wrong fight.

Greatness lies, not in being strong, but in the right using of strength; and strength is not used rightly when it serves only to carry a man above his fellows for his own solitary glory. He is the greatest whose strength carries up the most hearts by the attraction of his own.

Henry Ward Beecher

There are two kinds of people: those who say to God, "Thy will be done," and those to whom God says, "All right, then, have it your way."

C. S. Lewis

Do not be afraid to allow the Holy Spirit to reveal any unforgiveness or bitterness. The longer you hide it, the stronger it will become and the harder your heart will grow. Stay tenderhearted.

John Bevere

For Further Reflection

Psalm 111:10; Proverbs 2:6; James 3:13

TODAY'S PRAYER

Lord Jesus, I ask forgiveness for when I have wounded others in my need to be right. Help me to grow in my discernment, kindness, and wisdom in my journey to do your will. Thank you for your loving kindness. Amen.

Day 42

Jesus' Anger

*Jesus made a whip from some ropes and chased them
all out of the Temple. He drove out the sheep and cattle,
scattered the money changers' coins over the floor, and
turned over their tables. Then, going over to the people
who sold doves, he told them, "Get these things out of
here. Stop turning my Father's house into a marketplace!"*

JOHN 2:15–16

In any discussion among Christians on the subject of anger,
this passage of Jesus turning over the money tables is
usually brought up in defense of righteous anger. Jesus
was cleansing the temple of the money changers—those who
were using the temple to take advantage of worshipers by
overcharging for the animals needed for sacrifices. The money
changers were doing wrong, and Jesus was making it right.

Many things in life justify righteous anger, and we can use that
passion and energy to make positive changes in the world. But
if we aren't clear on our motives, our justified anger against
injustice and mistreatment can be misdirected and cause
more problems than it solves. Even justified anger can create a
lifetime of resentment and pain if we are unable to deal with it.

For instance, if we have experienced a terrible wrong or
injustice, that trauma can create anger that goes undetected
and can reverberate, causing extensive damage in our lives.
Jesus came so that we can have life. When he was turning
over the tables, he was correcting the wrong that was
happening. Because he is Jesus, he makes the wrongs right.

When you have experienced a wrong that has buried a rage inside, allow Jesus to turn that over and make it right, in his way and in his time. Although the wrong cannot be undone, the Lord can redeem that experience for good.

If you recognize that the anger you carry is unresolved pain, surrender it to Jesus. Even if you aren't ready to surrender it all, the simple acknowledgment that you have anger can begin to release the grip that it has on your life.

You cannot amputate your history from the fulfillment of your destiny. When I am in Jesus, my past is something he takes hold of and makes it into a destiny—that's called redemption!

Beth Moore

Anger and bitterness—whatever the cause—only ends up hurting us. Turn that anger over to Christ.

Billy Graham

For Further Reflection
1 Peter 5:8-9; Proverbs 28:16; Genesis 50:19-20

TODAY'S PRAYER
Lord Jesus, you know the fury that is within me from the offense against me. I offer it to you for healing and redemption. Turn the wrong into something that brings glory to your name. I don't want to carry it any longer. I trust you to make all things right in your time. Amen.

Day 43

Don't Give Up

So, let's not get tired of doing what is good. At just the right time we will reap a harvest of blessing if we don't give up.

GALATIANS 6:9

When you have been working diligently at something—whether it be school, your career, or a relationship—and it goes awry, it's upsetting, like watching one domino get knocked over, starting a chain reaction that undoes your hard work. You want to give up. You get angry because you tried to make sure everything was done correctly, and yet it all came crashing down.

Sometimes events happen that are out of your control and in anger and frustration, you might say, "Forget it! It's not worth it." People in a relationship might become so frustrated at feeling misunderstood or being taken advantage of that one or both of them give up, and the relationship ends. One person might be angry because they felt they did everything they could to save the relationship, but the relationship didn't work out and now they have to move on.

Anger can become an obstacle that stops people from moving forward in their lives, whether it be due to loss, misunderstandings, or disappointment. Overcome the feeling and make the choice today to seek help, restoration, and forgiveness.

Have you had anger prevent you from moving forward? Do you believe a relationship you're in cannot work out and you're done trying? Pray for insight to know how to overcome the obstacle anger created. Anger is a feeling, and feelings are not reliable or good at providing direction. Feelings change and cannot always be trusted. When you ask the Lord for help in resolving your anger, you can move forward and experience what God has for you.

It's hard to tell a great story if we remain stuck in chapter one.

Erwin Raphael McManus

We are told repeatedly in Scripture to prepare for hardships; so why do we believe our lives should be characterized by ease?

Patsy Clairmont

If you prayed as much as you complain and quarrel, you'd have a lot less to argue about and much more peace of mind.

Rick Warren

For Further Reflection
1 Corinthians 9:24; Isaiah 41:10; Hebrews 12:1–3

TODAY'S PRAYER
Lord God, you know how frustrating things can be. I pray for clarity to know how to proceed in the way you want me to go. Help me finish what needs to be finished in the way you want me to. Amen.

God First

*Seek the Kingdom of God above all else, and live
righteously, and he will give you everything you need.*

MATTHEW 6:33

One of the biggest challenges in dealing with anger is deciding, in that moment, whether you are going to give anger the control. Anger has a way of making you feel powerful. In your fury, you get loud, forceful, and sometimes physical. On some level, you begin to feel almost all-powerful. But if anger is controlling you, you're not the one in charge.

So how do you keep from relinquishing self-control in those moments and giving in to anger? First, ask yourself, is God first in my life? Seems like an odd question. You love God, so of course he is first. But maybe not. What does putting God first in your life look like? Humility, kindness, caring, righteous living, giving, and patience are a few examples. It's not that you will never experience anger or frustration, but it will not rule your life when God is first.

Second, recognize where anger is happening. Is it in a relationship? Maybe parenting is a challenge and you get frustrated and feel like screaming at the kids. If you recognize that your anger is taking over your life, ask God to intervene. Ask for help from trusted people who can offer assistance. Anger wants to rule your life, and it doesn't make a good god.

Lastly, a lot of anger comes from disappointment and sadness. Sometimes anger arises easily because you experienced anger from others. How has anger been influencing your life? Understanding where it comes from will help you as you begin to heal and move forward, allowing God to lead and direct your life. It is the best way to live!

You must ask for God's help. Even when you have done so, it may seem to you for a long time that no help, or less help than you need, is being given. Never mind. After each failure, ask forgiveness, pick yourself up, and try again. Very often what God first helps us towards is not the virtue itself but just this power of always trying again.

C. S. Lewis

Allow (stress) to dominate your life and you get chaos. Put God first and somehow everything falls into place. Scripture promises it.

Mariette Ulrich

Fervent prayer keeps your true identity in focus.

Priscilla Shirer

For Further Reflections

Philippians 3:14; Proverbs 14:12; Romans 12:19

TODAY'S PRAYER

Lord Jesus, thank you for saving me. My desire is to have you first in my life above all others. As I seek you first, help me to focus on your will for all of my days. I pray for clarity and understanding for your word. Thank you for your faithfulness! Amen.

Day 45

Wisdom

Sensible people control their temper;
they earn respect by overlooking wrongs.

Proverbs 19:11

How do we know when we need to address a wrongdoing or let it go? Offenses happen daily as a part of life, and many times letting them go is the obvious course of action and not too hard for us to do. But sometimes we need help discerning when we need to use our anger to work toward effecting a positive change, and when we need to process the anger, forgive, and move on.

Anger doesn't always mean shouting and rage. Sometimes anger is internalized and affects our patience and wisdom. We might not know how to express what we feel when an offense has occurred. In some cases, shock or overwhelming emotions can emotionally shut us down. In other instances, we might not be able to communicate our feelings well because of how we saw anger expressed (or repressed) in our families growing up.

Wisdom is needed in understanding which issues that are triggering anger need to be addressed. The anger that is felt doesn't always need to be resolved at the moment it occurs. For example, in a work situation, disagreement in policy might cause anger, but that anger can motivate us to take action, such as pursuing whether a new policy might be needed. If anger causes a blowup, it can cost us the job and allow a missed opportunity to make a positive change.

Discover where anger is residing internally and work on resolving it or using it to make the positive change that is needed. Ask the Lord to reveal where anger might be unresolved and to provide wisdom for each day.

God grant me the serenity to accept the things I cannot change, courage to change the things I can and the wisdom to know the difference.

Reinhold Niebuhr

When you are in conflict with someone, there is one factor that can make the difference between damaging your relationship and deepening it. That factor is attitude.

William James

May I govern my passions with absolute sway and grow wiser and better as life wears away.

Isaac Watts

For Further Reflection

Ephesians 5:15–16; James 3:17; Psalm 90:12

TODAY'S PRAYER

Lord Jesus, I pray for wisdom and patience. Help me to discern where unresolved bitterness and anger reside in me. I surrender the things I cannot resolve. Help me to address the things I can, with your grace and truth. Thank you for your power at work within me. Amen.

Day 46

Get Rid of It!

But now is the time to get rid of anger, rage, malicious behavior, slander, and dirty language.

COLOSSIANS 3:8

As we grow in faith, the things we say and do will need to change. This is the power of the Holy Spirit working in our hearts and minds. Reading the Bible, praying, and connecting with people all help us grow in faith, and the Holy Spirit moves in all of these things, helping us become more like Jesus.

In Colossians 3, the Apostle Paul provides a list of traits that have no place in this new life in Christ. Anger tops the list, followed by its "cousin" rage. Rage is the extreme of anger, it is revealed in behavior that is loud, violent, and uncontrolled. If we don't deal with anger, it can become rage—and sometimes both emotions are quietly lurking.

Road rage is a common example of the extreme of anger. People become furious because of a traffic issue, whether they got cut off, vehicles are moving too slowly, or some other traffic situation. The traffic didn't produce the rage; it revealed it. The driver who succumbs to road rage was already angry when they got into their car. They might not have been shouting or even looked angry, but when traffic didn't flow to their expectations, it uncovered what was below the surface.

Such behavior has to change. The rage that is felt toward other drivers, even if it doesn't leave the car, reveals what is in the heart. Yes, traffic is frustrating at times, but instead of an uncontrolled reaction, learn how to manage and respond in a better way.

In this same passage in Colossians, Paul encourages the reader to: "Put on your new nature and be renewed as you learn to know your Creator and become like him" (vs. 10). If you're not behaving in the way Jesus would, it's time to change.

I pray while driving. I pray while working, and while relaxing.

Joyce Meyer

God sees us as we are, loves us as we are, and accepts us as we are. But by his grace, he does not leave us as we are.

Timothy Keller

Provocation doesn't make me ill-tempered: it only shows me how ill-tempered I am.

C. S. Lewis

For Further Reflection

Titus 3:3–6; 1 Corinthians 5:7; Romans 12:1–2

TODAY'S PRAYER

Lord Jesus, thank you for your Holy Spirit at work within me. Help me to be sensitive to the direction and changes I need to make to become more like you. May my character reveal the work you have done in me. Amen.

Day 47

Be an Overcomer

Don't let evil conquer you,
but conquer evil by doing good.

ROMANS 12:21

What you feed grows; what you starve will eventually die. Addressing your anger will require time and patience. Unfortunately, if you have an issue with anger, you likely also have an issue with patience and might get frustrated at having to invest time to improve. But staying the same is not an option. So what can you do to start overcoming anger in your life?

Recognizing that anger is a problem is the first step. This happens when you stop blaming your anger on people and situations. People and situations can be frustrating and might never change. Your focus has to be on how you control your reaction to the inevitable. Instead of a big reaction the next time something angers you, make the decision—well ahead of time—to hold your reaction and respond better.

Second, take time to reflect on the last time your reaction was over the top. How would you want to respond if you could have a do-over? Many times, we replay what angered us and come up with more reactive things we would have said or done to win the conflict. That type of thinking is counterproductive. Instead, we have to think about what we could say or do next time that can lead toward a positive outcome. Set your mind on these reactions, and then begin practicing when minor issues occur. As you continue to practice responding differently, those reactions will become more instinctual, rather than anger.

Deciding not to let anger overcome you is a journey worth taking. To be in control of your anger will prevent a lifetime of misery, both for you and those around you. Every victory over uncontrolled anger is another step toward creating lasting change.

The only one you should compare yourself to is you. Your mission is to become better today than you were yesterday.

John C. Maxwell

I choose love. No occasion justifies hatred; no injustice warrants bitterness, I choose love. Today I will love God and what God loves.

Max Lucado

You cannot keep doing the same thing, the same way, and keep expecting something different to happen.

Beth Moore

For Further Reflection
James 1:2–4; Ephesians 6:13; 1 John 4:4

TODAY'S PRAYER
Lord, I know you are able to help me overcome the reactive nature of my anger. Help me as I surrender my will to yours so that I live my life for your glory. Amen

Love

And do everything with love.

1 Corinthians 16:14

It seems strange to talk about love and anger in the same sentence. However, many people who are in a relationship and love each other also experience anger with each other. Anger is passionate, and when a relationship is at an impasse on an issue, people often have strong reactions. Sadly, anger has destroyed love relationships.

People develop patterns in their relationships. This doesn't apply strictly to romantic relationships but also parent/child, employee/boss, and many other types of relationships. If a relationship has tension and results in anger, that anger can create a dynamic that continues throughout the life of the relationship. People keep score on who said what, and they try to retaliate to set the record straight. The relationship suffers as this habit eventually tears the connection apart.

The things that create anger and tension in relationships need to be discussed and resolved if possible. If resolution can't be found, the goal is to disagree respectfully. If the emotional temperature is too hot, give each other space and time before attempting to resolve the issue. Cover the situation in prayer and choose to do everything with love. What does that look like? It means not having to have the last word, not being easily offended, not having to settle the score, and many other loving responses.

Love does not mean ignoring problems but seeking to make things right instead of attacking the person. Working toward a solution can take significant effort and is more difficult than giving in to anger. A loving response requires patience, which is not always easy to have in the middle of a challenging situation. If love is the goal, finding the best way to deal with the things that create anger will change *everything*.

———————————

The will of God for your life is simply that you submit yourself to him each day and say, "Father, your will for today is mine. You lead me today and I will follow."

Kay Arthur

No form of vice, not worldliness, not greed of gold, not drunkenness itself, does more to un-Christianize society than evil temper.

Henry Drummond

When you resort to shouting in conflict, you are reacting in the flesh. You have lost control of the only person you can control: yourself.

Neil T. Anderson

———————————

For Further Reflection

Psalm 143:8; Proverbs 3:3–4; Ephesians 4:2

TODAY'S PRAYER

Lord Jesus, you are the greatest example of love. Help me to be more like you in every relationship and every response. I pray for discernment and wisdom when a conflict arises that I may reflect you. Amen

Peace

I have told you all this so that you may have peace in me.
Here on earth you will have many trials and sorrows.
But take heart, because I have overcome the world.

The opposite of anger is peace, where nothing is upsetting, out of order, or disturbing, when there is no score to settle or wrong to make right. Peace feels elusive when so many things are wrong in the world. We are surrounded by troubles—whether they be personal situations that cause pain and hardship or global conditions that create despair and anger. In the midst of these sorrows, Jesus offers peace that is eternal and not based on circumstances.

Circumstances often trigger anger to surface, which disrupts the peace. We might feel as though life is good until something goes off-kilter, upsetting us. And if we have an issue with anger, circumstances can go wrong more often than not. If that anger is internalized, we can find it difficult to experience peace because the root issue remains unresolved.

Do you long to have peace? What is disrupting peace for you? It could be tension in a relationship that has unresolved hurts. Maybe it is an injustice you have experienced. It could be a tremendous loss that feels unfair and has hollowed a space deep inside where anger has pooled.

To experience peace, we must resolve the areas in our life where hurt, fear, loss, injustice, and devastation have entered.

The way to peace is to surrender everything to Jesus. The process is through prayer, trusting that all things will work for good eventually, and deciding that anger will not take any more of your peace.

While you are proclaiming peace with your lips, be careful to have it even more fully in your heart.

St. Francis of Assisi

We are not at peace with others because we are not at peace with ourselves, and we are not at peace with ourselves because we are not at peace with God.

Thomas Merton

For Further Reflection

Isaiah 26:3; Proverbs 3:5-6; John 14:27

TODAY'S PRAYER

Lord God, I ask for peace in my heart. The things of this world have disrupted my peace, and I know I can only have true peace through you. I surrender to you the things I cannot fix, the sorrows I carry, and the challenges I will face. Help me cling to your true peace for all my days. In your name I ask, Amen.

Day 50

Patience vs. Power

Better to be patient than powerful; better to
have self-control than to conquer a city.

Think about the descriptions used for anger: "fly off the
handle," "blow up," "ticked off," "hot under the collar,"
"go ballistic," and "up in arms." These phrases provide
powerful visual images of what happens when anger is
expressed.

Anger, rage, and fury are powerful. Controlling those
emotions is easier for some people than for others. Giving in
to anger, rage, and fury can make you feel powerful in that
moment. But Proverbs 16 says it's better to be patient and
have self-control than it is to have power. Patience and self-
control are both characteristics of a Holy Spirit-filled life.

When God begins to work in your life, behaviors and
thinking that might have ruled your life before you became
a Christian begin to change. As you grow in your faith and
follow the Holy Spirit's leading, you are transformed to live
in a new way that reflects godliness. You will still have anger,
but it will not rule your life. You will grow in patience and
gain greater control of your reactions through God's strength
and power at work in you.

Continually surrender your life—and your emotions—to
God, and let the Holy Spirit do his refining work in you. In
so doing, you will experience increasing joy and peace in

the life God has for you. Spiritual growth requires time and patience, but the changes the Holy Spirit makes in your heart will empower you to live according to the higher calling God has for you. You will experience power in your life—a new power, fueled not by your own strength but by the energy God provides!

The wizard of Oz says look inside yourself and find self. God says look inside yourself and find the Holy Spirit. The first will get you to Kansas. The latter will get you to heaven. Take your pick.

Max Lucado

Growing up involves the work of the Holy Spirit forming our born-again spirits into the likeness of Christ.

Eugene H. Peterson

God will never direct us to be prideful, arrogant and unforgiving, immoral or slothful or full of fear. We step into these things because we are insensitive to the leadership of the Holy Spirit within us.

Charles Stanley

For Further Reflection
Romans 12:12; Isaiah 40:31; Ecclesiastes 7:8

TODAY'S PRAYER
Lord, I pray for the power of the Holy Spirit to produce patience in me. Help me to resist the urge to have my way, but instead yield to your way in me. Amen.

Day 51

Worthy of God's Calling

Therefore I, a prisoner for serving the Lord, beg you to lead a life worthy of your calling, for you have been called by God. Always be humble and gentle. Be patient with each other, making allowance for each other's faults because of your love.

EPHESIANS 4:1–2

When you accept Christ, you experience a true heart change. The Holy Spirit begins to work in your life, helping you to become more like Christ. This is a lifelong pursuit and requires your willingness to submit to God's plan for your life.

As Christ-followers, we are called to strive for godliness. In Ephesians 4, the Apostle Paul is writing from a prison cell, encouraging the believers to be the best they can be. How many of us are in a prison cell of our own making? Maybe we're confined by bitterness, resentment, or anger. Are we able to get free? Yes, by surrendering the "jailer" in our lives (any wound or offense) and allowing Jesus to free us. Relinquishing the wrong that was done to us and trusting that Jesus will one day make it right is the key to unlocking the cell we're in.

In the meantime, we have our own changes to make. The Bible teaches that what's inside our hearts eventually manifests in actions. If love is inside us, humility, gentleness, patience, kindness, and joy will be evident in our lives. If hate, resentment, guilt, shame, anger, and jealousy are within our hearts, those feelings eventually find their way out and into our relationships.

Are there things in your life that are keeping you imprisoned? Attitudes and behaviors that are not worthy of your calling? Perhaps anger is the most obvious, but what is below the surface? It needs to be worthy of the life God has called for you, because even though it might be hidden now, it will eventually be revealed in your life. Ask God to fill your heart with love so there will be no prison walls keeping you from enjoying your true freedom in Christ.

Stop introducing yourself to the next season of your life with the resume of your regrets from the last one.

Steven Furtick

Stone walls do not a prison make,/ Nor iron bars a cage;/ Minds innocent and quiet take/ That for an hermitage;/ If I have freedom in my love, and in my soul I am free,/ Angels alone, that soar above,/ Enjoy such liberty.

Richard Lovelace

For Further Reflection

Galatians 5:22–23; John 13:35; Romans 12:17–18

TODAY'S PRAYER

Lord Jesus, free me from the things that threaten my freedom in you. Help me to recognize where the bricks of anger and the iron bars of resentment seek to keep me from my calling. I ask this in your mighty name, Jesus. Amen

Pain of Anger

Even though I walk through the darkest valley,
I will fear no evil, for you are with me;
your rod and your staff, they comfort me.

Psalm 23:4 NIV

Have you ever cried angry tears? Or been so mad that it caused physical pain? Anger has many different expressions revealed in different forms of pain. Betrayal devastates; grief ravages; loss of a job or health create desperation. These experiences (and more) can create deep pain that can become expressed in anger.

Many times when we're in pain, we react in harmful and damaging ways—anything from screaming to physically hurting someone. Afterwards, the shame or guilt of our reaction causes us more pain. It seems like the pain of anger has its grip on us.

We are not immune to the effects of anger. There are moments in life when we will experience the full-on assault of pain, whether it is physical, emotional, mental, or spiritual. The pain of anger not only is felt in the moment of impact but also can reverberate inside our hearts and lives for years.

Do you recognize the pain of anger in your life? How does this pain get healed? By opening the wound, or at least acknowledging it is there. Pain that is rooted in anger can result in physical ailments as our bodies react to the emotional stress. Examples of physical effects include high blood pressure, headaches, and muscle and joint pain.

Effects of anger can take a toll on our mental health and create anxiety and depression. Spiritually, we can grow distant from God, not trusting him with the situation. As the places of pain are revealed, begin to work on healing them through prayer and counseling. Know that the healing process might cause more pain before it is done.

As you do the hard work of healing, be assured that God sees your pain. He knows the injustice you have experienced. He also knows the way out of the valley and will lead you to a better place if you will follow him.

Resentment is like a poison we carry around inside us with the hope that when we get the chance we can deposit it where it will harm another who has injured us.

Bert Ghezzi

Do not teach your children never to be angry; teach them how to be angry.

Lyman Abbott

We can ignore even pleasure. But pain insists upon being attended to.

C.S. Lewis

For Further Reflection
Psalm 91; 1 Peter 4:12-13; 2 Corinthians 1:3-4

TODAY'S PRAYER
Lord, my heart is hurting from the anger I feel. Please heal my heart and allow me to use the pain for good. Thank you for your strength and comfort. Amen.

Gentle Answer

A gentle answer deflects anger,
but harsh words make tempers flare.

PROVERBS 15:1

Think about the last time you raised your voice in anger. How does that memory make you feel? Does it bring up righteous indignation? Guilt? Shame? Controlling your anger involves restraining your impulses. You can learn to control your voice and the words you use when you're angry, but it won't happen automatically. How can you begin to have a gentle answer?

First, recognize that simply saying "I won't do that again" isn't enough. At some point in your life, after losing your temper, you've probably made a vow to yourself that you will be better next time. That promise alone isn't enough. Learn to recognize the indicators that you're getting angry. You might feel tension, hot around the collar, or your teeth clenching. The moment you begin to feel these warning signs, take note and choose to shift gears. You might have to say out loud, "I need to take a minute." Simply disrupting the momentum of your anger might make a huge difference. You can then take a moment (or several) to gain self-control and respond with an appropriate tone and answer.

Second, realize that any argument you are entering in a reactive state will not likely end well. Situations in life will make you angry, and you'll be tempted to raise your voice in frustration and rage. Learning how to express yourself in anger without creating more problems is a challenge, yet it's worth striving for.

Third, ask the Lord to help you make the change toward greater self-control. It's a matter of willingness to submit to how God wants you to respond to difficult situations. He is faithful to create a change in your heart and your response. You will be able to deal with the challenges in life without resorting to harsh words.

If you find that, despite all the efforts to forgive, your anger and bitterness cannot subside, you may need to look deeper and ask, "What am I defending? What is so important that I cannot live without?" It may be that, until some inordinate desire is identified and confronted, you will not be able to master your anger.

Tim Keller

It is wise to direct your anger towards problems—not people; to focus your energies on answers—not excuses.

William Arthur Ward

For Further Reflection

1 Peter 3:16; Proverbs 10:11; Matthew 15:11

TODAY'S PRAYER

Father God, hold my tongue when it wants to lash out at others. I want to control my words and use them for good. Help me to recognize when I am out of line with your desires for my life. In your name I ask, Amen

Day 54

Trusting God

I trust in you, my God! Do not let me be disgraced,
or let my enemies rejoice in my defeat.

PSALM 25:2

The Serenity Prayer by theologian Reinhold Niebuhr is said at recovery meetings, and by individuals seeking to find peace in their lives. Recovery is the process by which people heal their internal wounds, which have caused external challenges such as addiction but can also include other disruptions to our peace of mind and relationships.

If you struggle with anger, recovery is a process that will help you understand what is below the external expression of anger. You can take "steps" that will guide you toward healing and wholeness, no longer driven by anger.

Some people think recovery is only for drug and alcohol addiction. But when anything—substance, emotion, relationship, etc.—is directing our life, we need a path to healing. Some have referred to recovery as a sanctification process, clearing away the things in our lives that have replaced God. If you are tired of being controlled by anger, begin the process of recovery of your life today.

God, grant me the serenity
To accept the things I cannot change;
Courage to change the things I can,
And wisdom to know the difference.
Living one day at a time;
Enjoying one moment at a time;
Accepting hardship as the pathway to peace;
Taking, as He did, this sinful world
As it is, not as I would have it;
Trusting that He will make all things right
If I surrender to His will;
So that I may be reasonably happy in this life
And supremely happy with Him
Forever in the next. Amen.

Reinhold Niebuhr

For Further Reflection

1 Corinthians 6:12; John 8:36; Galatians 5:1

TODAY'S PRAYER

Lord Jesus, you have provided me freedom. Help me no longer be enslaved by anger or anything else. Thank you for your redeeming power that is at work in me. Help me be willing to do whatever you call me to do, trusting that you will make all things right. Amen.

Day 55

Resistance

So humble yourselves before God.
Resist the devil, and he will flee from you.

JAMES 4:7

One challenge with anger is that, in and of itself, it is not wrong or a sin. It is a very important part of our lives, which expresses displeasure at things we experience and can motivate us to make changes. However, when anger becomes manager of our lives, it becomes a tool of the enemy to potentially destroy us. How can this God-given emotion become a destructive tool of the devil? With our help!

When we allow anger to settle in, it begins to drive our lives. It takes us places we never planned to go. It ruins relationships, careers, and ministries. Anger often lies below the surface and looks like depression, criticism, isolation, and divisiveness. Anger might not be at full force when it is tucked away, but is a motivator and can cause reactions that aren't godly. How do we know if this is happening in our lives? We probably already know, but if we don't, someone close to us knows.

As followers of Christ, we are called to a better life, one that is not controlled by anything but the Holy Spirit of God. When anger is controlling us, we must resist it and ask God to help. Anger has the power to overcome our lives, but God is more powerful, and when we allow God to do whatever is necessary to clean our heart, he is faithful and will do it. With his help, we can experience anger but not be controlled by it.

Begin today to resist the enemy, and the enemy will flee! As you experience life without anger, you will experience joy and peace, and so will the people you are around. You will have a lightness in your spirit, living in the way God designed you to live.

The only thing necessary for the triumph of evil is for good men to do nothing.

Edmund Burke

The battleline between good and evil runs through the heart of every man.

Aleksandr Solzhenitsyn

The devil will give up when he sees that you are not going to give in.

Joyce Meyer

For Further Reflection

Jeremiah 29:11; Joshua 1:9; Psalm 32:8

TODAY'S PRAYER

Lord Jesus, I humbly ask for your strength to resist the enemy's attacks. Help me to use anger in a way that you designed it to be used. I ask for my life to reflect you and be used for your glory. In your name I ask, Amen.

Day 56

Great Hope!

*For his anger lasts only a moment, but his favor lasts
a lifetime! Weeping may last through the night,
but joy comes with the morning.*

PSALM 30:5

The things that make us angry can overwhelm, even overtake, our lives. The effects of the devastating betrayals, frustrating situations, and gut-wrenching losses can last longer than we ever expected. These experiences often become the whole narrative of our lives as we retell the unbelievable but true stories.

When these things happen, we often go to the Lord and ask—no, plead—for relief, for answers, and for restitution. We wrestle with the "why," knowing there is no answer that will make any sense of the situation, which leads to more frustration, anger, and devastation. How could this terrible event have happened? When will any of this make sense or be made right? Hope is lost and anger remains.

God knows what we go through and will provide strength and peace for our lives. The promise of redemption is ours for every situation in which we feel betrayed, grief, and injustice. We must continue to seek God in the most difficult times when we would rather get even or stay resentful for a lifetime.

We can have great hope in God's plan to make all things right in his perfect will and time. We might not be able to make sense of things this side of heaven, but as we lean in and trust God with the details, he will provide peace and security—and even joy instead of anger.

What are you staying angry about? Will you follow God's plan? Feel the anger, pain, and sorrow, and then give it to the Lord. He is our great hope!

True healing will not finally come from identifying causes or assigning guilt, but from trusting God.

Marshall Segal

To be a Christian means to forgive the inexcusable, because God has forgiven the inexcusable in you.

C.S. Lewis

When we give in to resentment, we act in self-destructive ways and hurt ourselves much more than those we're holding grudges against.

Rick Warren

For Further Reflection

Matthew 5:44; Hebrews 12:14–15; Mark 9:23

TODAY'S PRAYER

Father God, this world has brought pain into my life, and I need help getting through it. Help me release my anger and hurt to you, because you are the only one who can make all things right. You are my hope. I ask for your peace and strength daily in my life. Amen.

Top Ten

You must not murder.

Exodus 20:13

The Ten Commandments are a set of rules that God hand-wrote for Moses as he was leading the children of Israel to the Promised Land. They were an unruly bunch, much as we are, and needed God's guidance desperately. None of the Ten Commandments explicitly lists anger in it. Yet one of the commandments does say, "You must not murder." It might seem like a big stretch from anger to murder, but then again it really isn't.

In the Sermon on the Mount, Jesus talked about the commandments, but he focused his disciples' attention on the root issue—our sinful hearts. He said, "'You have heard that our ancestors were told, "You must not murder. If you commit murder, you are subject to judgment." But I say, if you are even angry with someone, you are subject to judgment!'" (Matthew 5:21–22).

Murder begins in the heart. Anger is the seed. When anger takes root and begins to affect every area of a person's life, it can destroy lives. Anger connects to many other feelings and expressions, including tears, loud verbal assaults, and worse. When these strong feelings continue to be fueled, murder isn't that far off. If you are feeling this angry, seek help immediately. The seeds of murder begin in anger and need to be uprooted and cleared out.

Life is not meant to be lived stuck in anger. God knows the sinfulness of the human heart and our tendency to wander down the wrong paths. Long ago, he set in place the rules to lead us in the right direction. If anger wants to route you down the wrong road, stop and turn around today.

An attitude can murder just as easily as an ax.

Woodrow Kroll

God longs for us to freely pour out every single emotion, no matter how toxic, right before him.

Beth Moore

Because of Calvary, I'm free to choose. And so I choose. I choose love.... No occasion justifies hatred, no injustice warrants bitterness.

Max Lucado

For Further Reflection

1 John 3:11–12; Proverbs 6:16–18; John 10:10

TODAY'S PRAYER

Lord, cleanse me of any anger that threatens to overtake me. Heal the wounds from the past and help me forgive and be free to live for you. The offense that wants to enslave me is not worth the cost of my freedom. Forgive me and set me free. Amen.

Prayer Works!

But I say, love your enemies! Pray for those who persecute you! In that way, you will be acting as true children of your Father in heaven. For he gives his sunlight to both the evil and the good, and he sends rain on the just and the unjust alike.

MATTHEW 5:44–45

When we're attacked or wronged by someone, our instinct is to retaliate. The obsessive thinking that accompanies anger is fuel for the flame, and it blinds us. We get so laser-focused on the wrongdoing, who did it, and our plan of attack that we forget that Jesus called us to a better life.

Many of us are fighting battles every day using useless weapons that eventually cause our defeat. Jesus' method is opposite the natural inclinations of our sinful nature—love our enemies and pray for them. These are probably the last weapons we would reach for in the battle, yet it is the way God has for us to live.

What does this look like in real time? The biggest weapon is to stop before reacting. This will be the most difficult but over time will become easier. When we learn to control our reactive nature, we can be responsive to the issue, not lash out against the person. In this way, we are loving our enemies, not engaging with weapons that are of our old nature, which can be hateful. Taking a pause and exercising self-control will open us to be able to pray for our enemies and address the problem to gain an outcome that honors Christ.

Through the power of prayer, the Word of God, and the Holy Spirit, we are better suited for the battles of this life. As we pray for peace in our hearts and in this world, God is faithful to provide exactly what we need to be victorious!

To me, it has been a source of great comfort and strength in the day of battle, just to remember that the secret of steadfastness, and indeed, of victory, is the recognition that "the Lord is at hand."

Duncan Campbell

There's nothing more calming in difficult moments than knowing there's someone fighting with you.

Mother Teresa

We pray because our own solutions don't work and because prayer deploys, activates, and fortifies us against the attacks of the enemy. We pray because we're serious about taking back the ground he has sought to take from us.

Priscilla Shirer

For Further Reflection
Jeremiah 29:12-13; Psalm 17:6; James 1:19-20

TODAY'S PRAYER
Lord Jesus, equip me for the battles I will face today. Help me lay down my weapons from past conflicts that may have created bitterness in me. Lead me as I encounter threats, knowing that you have provided your Holy Spirit to help me be victorious each day. Amen.

Forgiveness

Make allowance for each other's faults, and forgive
anyone who offends you. Remember, the Lord
forgave you, so you must forgive others.

COLOSSIANS 3:13

When we are upset about something, irritated and frustrated about a situation, we sometimes take the approach, "My mind is made up; don't confuse me with the facts." We don't want to hear any explanations or excuses and become irate if the other person wants to offer their side of the situation.

How's that working for you? When you think about the situation, does it take you right back to the point of impact? You believe the anger you felt about the situation was justified, and even if you heard all the details, you might still have residual anger to deal with. That anger can become depression as you stuff the emotion deep inside. You might also begin to experience anxious thoughts as the fury subsides but the echoes of it remain.

The remedy is forgiveness. You might think the injustice you experienced is the unforgivable offense, but in God's design, there is no such thing. Forgiveness is for you, not the offender. You can be free to heal and move forward in your life. It doesn't mean you have to forget the offense and resume the relationship. Rather, it means you have accepted that it did happen and have forgiven the offender in order to let it go. This is the pathway for freedom.

What are you holding onto? Does your anger stir when you recall the offense? It's time to let it go and start living your life free of the past. Begin to take steps to heal the wound and to move into the present, no longer governed by what happened. God forgave you, and you can forgive others because of this forgiveness.

To forgive is to set a prisoner free and discover that the prisoner was you.

Lewis B. Smedes

We think that forgiveness is weakness, but it's absolutely not; it takes a very strong person to forgive.

T. D. Jakes

For Further Reflection

Luke 6:37; Matthew 18:21–22; Psalm 103:12

TODAY'S PRAYER

Father God, I am struggling with anger about the wrong that happened to me. I wrestle with how to make sense of it or make the person pay for what they have done. Help me move into your forgiveness for them and for the offense. I want to be free of this anger and not allow bitterness to take root in my life. Thank you for your forgiveness! Amen.

Day 60

Following the Leader

Teach me how to live, O Lord. Lead me along
the right path, for my enemies are waiting for me.

PSALM 27:11

Who or what is leading your life? Is anger in charge? If so, how can you tell? Anger can go undetected for years. But if you ask those closest to you, "How have you seen anger displayed in my life?" you might get some insight. You can also ask God to reveal where anger is controlling you. You might already know how anger has been affecting your life and want to make changes. Now is the time!

Anger is a necessary and vital emotion. It is a warning system to indicate our boundaries have been crossed, betrayal has occurred, or expectations have been unmet. Without it, we would be in a terrible mess! It is so important to know anger is not wrong when it fulfills its intended purpose. But it takes skill to determine when anger has become the problem instead of anger alerting you to a problem.

What you do with your anger also is a learned skill. As a toddler you learned the powerful word no and used it often as you exercised your power. However, as you mature, you have to learn how to control your anger and use it in healthy ways. Learning to express anger in a way that will help you function in life is a valuable skill that might need refining.

Learning to follow the right leader, the Lord God, learning new ways to cope when things go wrong, learning to express anger in healthy ways, and learning where anger is trying to lead are valuable lessons. Recognizing you still have things to learn about your anger is an indicator you are on the right path.

———————▸———————

God has gone before us so we can walk in the future he has for us.

Priscilla Shirer

God uses change to change us. He doesn't use it to destroy us or to distract us, but to coax us to the next level of character, experience, compassion and destiny!

Beth Moore

It is not about doing what we feel like. It is about doing what God says.

Joyce Meyer

———————▸———————

For Further Reflection

John 14:26; Deuteronomy 5:33; Psalm 119:3

TODAY'S PRAYER

Lord Jesus, I want to follow you all the days of my life! Help me to grow in your wisdom and discernment. Show me the path that you desire for me so that I may not be ruled by anything other than you. For your glory and in your name I pray, Amen.

Day 61

Better Wisdom

Trust in the Lord with all your heart;
do not depend on your own understanding.

PROVERBS 3:5

L ife does not always make sense. When an event happens
that is confusing, painful, or complex, we want to
know why it is the way it is and we want to know now.
Sometimes we simply cannot accept what happened and are
angry about it. It just doesn't make sense that a loving God
would allow something so obviously wrong to happen.

This passage from Proverbs is usually paired with the verse
that follows: "Seek his will in all you do, and he will show you
which path to take." However, let's sit with verse 5 for a bit
longer. Sometimes we need to work more on trusting the Lord
fully and not depending on our own wisdom before we start
trying to figure out what's next on the path he's put us on.

Sometimes life itself can seem like a giant jigsaw puzzle. The
edge pieces are life and death, and the picture has so many
different colors, shapes, and sizes, it takes the wisdom of the
Lord to understand a little better how the completed puzzle
will look!

God provides wisdom through his word, prayer, and people.
Beginning to trust God is a step in a long journey. He knows
where we are going, and he is trustworthy and wise. In the
process of surrendering, we will grow in our trust in God,
through experiencing his faithfulness and wisdom. As we

continue to trust God with *all* things, we will have peace that he is working amid the confusion. He provides better wisdom!

My trust in God flows out of the experience of his loving me, day in and day out, whether the day is stormy or fair, whether I'm sick or in good health, whether I'm in a state of grace or disgrace. He comes to me where I live and loves me as I am.

Brennan Manning

God's piecing together the puzzle of your life and He's filling what's still missing with His peace.

Ann Voskamp

When you know what God says, what he means, and how to put his truths into practice, you will be equipped for every circumstance of life.

Kay Arthur

For Further Reflection
James 3:17; Ephesians 5:15-17; Psalm 111:10

TODAY'S PRAYER
Thank you God for your wisdom! Help me to trust you more each day. Help me recognize when I am trying to replace your wisdom with my own and lead me in your path. In your name, Amen.

Day 62

Gift of Peace

I am leaving you with a gift—peace of mind and heart.
And the peace I give is a gift the world cannot give.
So don't be troubled or afraid.

JOHN 14:27

No one likes unpleasant surprises. But the unexpected happens—regularly. And it can cause us to lose our temper as well as our sense of peace. Too often our peace is determined by our ability to control our circumstances.

The peace that Jesus provides is not based on circumstances being what we expect, or all things lining up. It is based on the One who overcame death and is still working in our lives through the power of the Holy Spirit. This peace comes as we learn that no matter what we are going through, the Lord Jesus goes before us and will be our rear guard. We don't have control of circumstances and have to learn how to navigate the uncertainty.

Uncertainty and control are two triggers for anger. Circumstances get disrupted, we face the unknown, and tempers flare. In that moment, we have to lean on the power of the Holy Spirit, stop the reaction, take a breath, and realize we don't have to let these events steal our peace. If our peace is based on Christ, it cannot be moved. Our peace might be challenged, and we will definitely have strong feelings about the situation, but we can learn how to release the feelings and seek the Lord for his guidance.

Peace is a gift. Anyone can stay calm when everything is going right. It takes God's strength working in us to keep that peace when things are crazy. We need the Prince of Peace to work in our lives in the midst of the constant change we experience. When we get angry when life goes haywire, we can deal with it from a place of peace. What a gift!

Because of the empty tomb, we have peace. Because of his resurrection, we can have peace during even the most troubling of times because we know he is in control of all that happens in the world.

Paul Chappell

Christ alone can bring lasting peace — peace with God — peace among men and nations — and peace within our hearts.

Billy Graham

God is in control, and therefore in EVERYTHING I can give thanks—not because of the situation but because of the One who directs and rules over it.

Kay Arthur

For Further Reflection

Philippians 4:6–7; 2 Thessalonians 3:16; Isaiah 26:3

TODAY'S PRAYER

Lord Jesus, thank you for your gift of peace! I will open and use this gift every day to your glory. Help me to stay in your peace regardless of what is happening, knowing that you are working in all things for the good. Amen.

Day 63

Sleep on It

Don't sin by letting anger control you.
Think about it overnight and remain silent.

PSALM 4:4

We will experience anger throughout our lives, but the reactions we have when we are angry can create a new set of problems. Some people have bigger reactions than other people do. Personalities, habits, and family "traditions" all affect the way we express our anger. But even those who quietly seethe in anger will discover that anger can take control.

When we create drama in our anger, it usually entails yelling, screaming, caustic remarks, and physical reactions such as throwing things, physically accosting others, and causing property damage. If you have reacted like this in your anger, you probably have guilt for the wrong you have done and shame from your reaction. Anger has successfully controlled you. But it doesn't have to have control of you forever.

Controlling your anger will change your life for the better. Sin, no matter the cause, destroys life. That is why Jesus died and rose again, defeating death so that sin cannot have the last word. If your anger has caused you to sin, ask for forgiveness, from God and from anyone who was affected by your reaction.

Anger needs expression in a positive way, not the reactive, out-of-control way. Positive expressions of anger can include deep breathing, journaling, having a productive conversation with the other person, and bringing a resolution to the problem in a peaceful way.

When you become angry, take a breath or, as Psalm 4:4 recommends, "Think about it overnight and remain silent." In many Bible translations this passage is followed by the word "Selah" or "Interlude," meaning "take a break." Practice putting space between your emotion and your reaction. In this way, you can begin to control your anger.

Trust God to take care of you in all circumstances. Do you realize what the enemy will lose if you surrender and trust God?

Beth Moore

I choose gentleness... Nothing is won by force. I choose to be gentle. If I raise my voice may it be only in praise. If I clench my fist, may it be only in prayer. If I make a demand, may it be only of myself.

Max Lucado

For Further Reflection
Titus 1:7; Leviticus 19:17–18; Proverbs 27:3

TODAY'S PRAYER
Lord Jesus, help me to pause before I react. Help me to wait upon you for your direction and wisdom. And help me control my anger so that it doesn't control me. I want to reflect your love and grace in my life. Amen.

Heart of the Matter

*Guard your heart above all else, for it determines
the course of your life.*

PROVERBS 4:23

M atters of the heart are the heart of what's the matter. Many people experience life-changing trauma that changes the way they live. Trauma in the original Greek means "wound." Think of how your heart might have been wounded, and you will discover where healing needs to take place. Anger is a common trauma response, as well as anxiety and depression, along with other emotional, physical, and spiritual responses to trauma. Someone who has experienced trauma might have moved on from the initial wound, but the infection, figuratively speaking, continues to affect them.

Anger as a trauma response is an over-the-top reaction to a situation that is not the initial wound. You might have moved on from the first cut, but the pain continues beneath the surface. It might be touched on when something minor occurs, causing you to react disproportionately to the incident.

For trauma to be resolved, it must be processed, which can feel scary. To open a wound that seemingly has healed is painful and requires support. But processing the trauma can mean complete healing for something that otherwise has the potential to take over your life. Resolving the pain will provide the healing needed for your heart.

Could something from the past be triggering your anger? Think about the last time your anger was a bit out of context for what was happening in the moment. It might indicate that your heart needs healing. You will need to ask for help from a skilled clinician who can provide a safe place for trauma healing. Asking God to provide healing for our hearts will give us the ability to live in the present. To live whole-heartedly is a gift of God and one worth opening.

———————▶———————

The work of restoration cannot begin until a problem is fully faced.

Dan Allender

When we can talk about our feelings, they become less overwhelming, less upsetting, and less scary. The people we trust with that important talk can help us know that we are not alone.

Fred Rogers

God wants you to be delivered from what you have done and from what has been done to you. Both are equally important to him.

Joyce Meyer

———————▶———————

For Further Reflection
Psalm 107:13–16; Isaiah 41:10; Matthew 11:28–30

TODAY'S PRAYER
Lord Jesus, help me as I reveal my wounds and offer them up for healing. Help me to trust that you will provide helpers for my healing as I reach out. Amen.

No Paybacks

*Don't repay evil for evil. Don't retaliate with insults
when people insult you. Instead, pay them back with
a blessing. That is what God has called you to do,
and he will grant you his blessing.*

1 Peter 3:9

The things that make you angry often create an urge to retaliate. You might think it will help you feel better about the hurt done to you or someone you love. But vengeance does not remedy the original wrong. When you accept this truth, you can learn how to deal with wrongs in a way that God desires. The new life God calls you to is one of self-control, and he provides the Holy Spirit to help you in your time of pain and struggle. God is faithful, and when you allow him to work, you can resist paying back evil for evil.

You might be thinking, "You don't realize what happened" or "It's only fair that they get what they deserve." Pray to change your mindset. Very little is fair when it comes to being the victim of someone's bad treatment. Wrong is just wrong. That's why your focus has to turn toward how God wants you to respond. Sometimes walking away is best—it untangles you from the offender and prevents you from reacting in a way that is not godly. Walking away is not easy, and you might need help changing your thought process to be able to truly let go of what happened.

Refusing to retaliate doesn't mean you approve of what happened or that it didn't affect you. You will need to work through the pain and forgive the offense—and it will take time. As you strengthen your ability to not retaliate and instead focus on doing what God wants, you will experience the blessing of peace in your life. That is the best payback of all.

Temper is what gets most of us into trouble. Pride is what keeps us there.

Mark Twain

If you believe in a God who controls the big things, you have to believe in a God who controls the little things. It is we, of course, to whom things look "little" or "big."

Elisabeth Elliot

What gives me the most hope every day is God's grace; knowing that his grace is going to give me the strength for whatever I face, knowing that nothing is a surprise to God.

Rick Warren

For Further Reflection
Ephesians 4:26–27; Proverbs 14:16–17; Romans 12:21

TODAY'S PRAYER
Lord God, you know the offense that I have experienced. I ask for your supernatural strength as I resist the urge to react. May I have the ability to trust you to make all things right in your time and experience your blessing of peace as I follow your will. Amen.

Day 66

Focus

You will keep in perfect peace all who trust in you,
all whose thoughts are fixed on you!

ISAIAH 26:3

The brain is an amazing organ! So complex and creative, it is the holder of your memories, thoughts, and ideas and is the operating system of your body. The brain's warning system is instinctive and powerful and helps you escape danger. When you experience a perceived threat, your brain respond with fight, flight, or freeze.

Your brain can also get stuck in one of the three responses, meaning the way in which you respond to a perceived threat can become a pattern in your brain. Unfortunately, if you have experienced trauma, *everything* can appear as a threat, triggering false alarms in your warning system, causing multiple problems in your life and relationships.

There is help! First, recognize you will need help getting unstuck. A counselor or psychiatrist might be able to help you identify the source of the problem. Second, learn new ways to deal with your anger, such as redirecting your thoughts, meditating on God's word, taking a step back before reacting, and creating new strategies that will keep you calmer. Third, begin to be aware of when you might be stuck. Professional help might not always be needed; sometimes connecting with a trusted friend or loved one and talking about what you are feeling can be powerful and productive.

As you meditate on the word of God and it becomes part of your thinking, you can experience peace. When you can learn how to calm your thoughts and are able to stay focused, your brain benefits too! You have been created by an amazing God who provides peace that passes understanding!

If we have not quiet in our minds, outward comfort will do no more for us than a golden slipper on a gouty foot.

John Bunyan

A great many people are trying to make peace, but that has already been done. God has not left it for us to do; all we have to do is to enter into it.

D.L. Moody

Peace comes in situations completely surrendered to the sovereign authority of Christ.

Beth Moore

For Further Reflection
John 16:33; 2 Corinthians 13:11; Psalm 4:8

TODAY'S PRAYER
Lord, you have created me and know me inside and out. I ask for your healing power in my mind, soul, and body. Show me where I may be stuck and lead me to the helpers in my journey. I pray that as you work in me that I will experience your peace. Amen.

Day 67

Practice, Practice, Practice

Keep putting into practice all you learned and received from me—everything you heard from me and saw me doing. Then the God of peace will be with you.

PHILIPPIANS 4:9

Where do you recognize negative habits, specifically reactive anger, in your life? Maybe you're prone to road rage, shouting at other drivers, blowing your horn, or behaving in other aggressive ways. You'll have to take deliberate steps to change this bad habit. It would be great if self-control were automatic, if you didn't have to do anything differently and could be calm, cool, and collected. But self-control doesn't just happen; it's something you have to keep practicing to develop.

How can you grow in self-control? If you recognize you have a problem with road rage, begin by recognizing that all drivers are imperfect, including you. Then when you get behind the wheel, create space for the things that will go wrong, driving offensively as you were probably taught in driver's training. Pay attention to your thoughts toward the other drivers. Are you calling them names? They might not hear you (hopefully). But you—and others in the car—can hear you, and your words are powerful. Negative feelings toward other people will affect you negatively. Catch your negative thoughts and replace them with positive ones. Then practice, practice, practice. Before long, you will be able to have a positive driving experience!

Apply these principles in whatever area you find yourself struggling. Perhaps your parenting style needs help. Are you yelling instead of having conversations? At work, are you fueled by anger and frustrated by your coworkers? It could be time to create new habits, ones that will need practicing but eventually will become automatic.

What is your anger habit? It's time to break it. Through the power of the Holy Spirit and practicing new ways to deal with anger, we will experience self-control and the peace of God.

Small disciplines done consistently lead to big results over time.

Craig Groeschel

Discipline is doing what needs to be done even when you don't want to do it.

Zig Ziglar

Obedience is less painful than regret.

Christine Caine

For Further Reflection
1 Timothy 4:15; Romans 8:6; Psalm 34:14

TODAY'S PRAYER
Lord Jesus, I surrender to your plan and will practice the way you have desired for my life. Help me as I begin to make changes that will help my life reflect you in every area. I pray for the power of your Holy Spirit to be working in me. Amen.

Finish Well

So get rid of all evil behavior. Be done with all deceit,
hypocrisy, jealousy, and all unkind speech.

1 PETER 2:1

When you look at your past, you might remember times when rage filled your days, and guilt and shame can overwhelm you. You want a different life, one not defined by anger and fury.

Maybe you've experienced someone else's anger, having witnessed many tirades and blowups that were scary and sad. Maybe you've exhibited your own rage and fury and been surprised and regretful afterwards, either because of how you acted or because you're frustrated that situations in your life are not improving. How can you do better with anger?

Decide today to make one change in the way you express anger. For example, if you are prone to raising your voice when you get angry, decide you will not do that any longer. It is possible for you to do this. If you were in church and got angry, you probably wouldn't give in to shouting. If you tend to keep your anger inside until you eventually blow up, decide to address the feelings of anger in the moment. It can be as simple as saying "I feel angry about ____." The situation might not have immediate resolution, but expressing your anger in the moment can keep you from burying the emotion inside only to have it rise later.

You can change! Anger is a necessary emotion that you can learn to control. Begin today by making one decision toward the goal of changing your expression of anger. Accept that things will come up that will make you angry, but be confident that you can respond in a healthy way and finish well!

Is all anger sin? No, but some of it is. Even God himself has righteous anger against sin, injustice, rebellion, and pettiness.

Joyce Meyer

The emotions of anger and fear are reactions to threatening situations or people. Love is the emotion of self-control, for when love is our response, we are able to act, not react, to life.

Dr. David Stoop

Now I am making an end of my anger. It does not become me, unrelentingly to rage on.

Home

For Further Reflection

Romans 13:14; 1 Timothy 3:2; Philippians 1:27

TODAY'S PRAYER

Lord, I want to have control of my temper. Help me to reflect you in my responses. When anger arises, help me to use it in the way you design and to find resolution where possible. Amen.

Prayer

*Keep watch and pray, so that you will not give in to
temptation. For the spirit is willing, but the body is weak!*

MATTHEW 26:41

When you are facing a challenge that seems insurmountable, you can have faith that God is working in your situation for the good. Some people mistakenly expect that a follower of Christ will not have any difficulties in life. But along the journey, you will experience many trials and adversities. However, you can know that God will help you through even the most difficult times.

Anger might be the way you have been reacting to the troubles in your life. When you are dealing with something that isn't fair or feels like you are being attacked, anger can make you feel in control of the situation. However, anger is only an emotional reaction to the situation; it isn't a solution to the problem.

So instead of anger, what strategy can you use to cope with difficulty? Prayer. Talk to God in the moment of anger, but also spend time each day talking with him about your struggles and challenges. When we're angry about something, it can be difficult to quiet ourselves and seek God in prayer. We can be so focused on what went wrong, what is unfair, or how it all happened that we don't even give prayer a second thought. When we really need to pray, instead we often revert to our old ways of coping with life.

Begin today to pray about what makes you angry. Share with God the pain, anger, sorrow, and fear. Prayer doesn't have to be on your knees or with fancy words. It could be, "Help me, Lord." God wants to hear from you, because he loves you and cares about your life.

Prayer is the exercise of drawing on the grace of God.

Oswald Chambers

Prayer is not monologue, but dialogue; God's voice is its most essential part. Listening to God's voice is the secret of the assurance that he will listen to mine.

Andrew Murray

When your spirit is heavy, when your heart is broken, when your burdens seem unbearable—trust him. Look to him.

Anne Graham Lotz

For Further Reflection

1 John 5:14–15; 2 Chronicles 7:14; Ephesians 6:18

TODAY'S PRAYER

Lord Jesus, I am burdened with the challenges I face and feel overwhelmed. You are able to provide a way and I am willing to do what you desire. Thank you that you are always there for me! Your strength and wisdom are what I need to face the day. Thank you for your love and grace to see me through. Amen.

Day 70

Hope In Christ

O Lord, you are so good, so ready to forgive,
so full of unfailing love for all who ask for your help.

PSALM 86:5

Have you ever been blinded by anger? So enraged by the injustice or threat that you lose sight of the bigger picture?

When we experience something that is traumatic, we can get stuck. Since our pain is justified, we stay in that place of anger, unaware that healing is available and regardless of the pain it causes. Some of what we think and say might be true. The wrong against us might have been horrible. But if we fixate on the person who is to blame and continue to live in the past, we will be unable to see that there is hope for healing.

Some things that happen have no explanation. Evil exists in the world, and sometimes we experience it personally. It is appropriate to have anger toward such things. Our healing process is to release our anger in a healthy way and move forward in our lives. We might not be able to forget what happened, but the anger can subside, and our vision can focus on the future rather than trying to rearrange the past.

Forgiveness is a part of the healing journey and lets us have a healthy relationship with the past. We forgive to release us from the past and move forward in our lives. We might not forget what happened, but it won't have the power to blind us to the present and future.

Begin today by forgiving, healing and moving forward free of the anger that binds you to the past. You will have a clear view of the hope you have in Christ!

Focus on giants – you stumble. Focus on God – giants tumble.

Max Lucado

Forgiveness is an act of the will, and the will can function regardless of the temperature of the heart.

Corrie ten Boom

To love means loving the unlovable. To forgive means pardoning the unpardonable. Faith means believing the unbelievable. Hope means hoping when everything seems hopeless.

G.K. Chesterton

For Further Reflection
Romans 12:17; Ephesians 4:31-32; Matthew 18:21-22

TODAY'S PRAYER
Lord Jesus, my heart is hurting because of the wrong I have experienced. Help me to let go and forgive to be free from the resentment that wants to entangle my life. Amen.

Distressed

From the depths of despair, O Lord, I call for your help.
Hear my cry, O Lord. Pay attention to my prayer.

Psalm 130:1–2

When something has troubled our souls and we are angry, we can feel as though the Lord doesn't care or isn't listening. The situation or person isn't changing fast enough, the wrong cannot be undone, and we have asked God to intervene, but nothing has changed.

Sometimes we get frustrated, even angry with God, because he doesn't seem anywhere around. In times of desperation, when we believe the lie that we are on our own and God doesn't care, we feel angry that we're facing the struggle alone. The truth is God is always with us. He hears our prayers and is working on our behalf. We have to seek God in prayer, wait on Him, and trust he will work all things out.

When we are fretting about a situation, frustrated and angry, it can be difficult to pray. It feels like prayer isn't enough— action needs to be taken. When we are fueled by anger and desperation, we want to fix the problem. But in those times, prayer is essential. We have to seek the Lord's will, express our concerns and anger, and ask God for direction. The hard part is that the answer might be to wait.

God is near and hears, even when it seems he is not working. Trust and pray, knowing he will be your guide. Share your burdens with trusted friends and loved ones, asking them to pray for you and with you. Spend time in the Bible. These actions are the best steps to take in the tough places. God hears you.

Not to pray because you do not feel fit to pray is like saying, "I will not take medicine because I am too ill." Pray for prayer: pray yourself, by the Spirit's assistance, into a praying frame.

Charles Spurgeon

Prayer is where the action is.

John Wesley

Whatever has you afraid, angry, intimidated or frustrated tonight – take it to our all-powerful and all-capable God. He has the answer.

Lysa TerKeurst

For Further Reflection

Philippians 4:6–7; 2 Chronicles 6:21; Mark 11:24

TODAY'S PRAYER

Thank you, Lord, for hearing me even when I doubt. Help me to trust in you more and lean into your strength and wisdom for my situation. Thank you for your loving care for me. Amen.

Day 72

Harmony

So then, let us aim for harmony in the church
and try to build each other up.

ROMANS 14:19

I f you are a believer in Christ, you are most likely part
of a local church. This is a very important part of your
faith journey and such a great blessing in your walk with
Christ. Being in a community of fellow believers worshiping
and serving God together can be wonderful.

However, the enemy's interference can create heartbreaking
losses. How can a group of people who love and serve God
become adversaries? You might have witnessed this or maybe
you are experiencing it now. Someone gets angry—and it
could be justified anger—and then people take sides. Before
you know it, there is a split in the church. Both sides are
hurting, angry, and certain they are in the right.

How do we address anger within the church? After all, church
is full of imperfect people who are still being conformed to
Christ's image and often have not surrendered to his will.
The Bible offers advice on how to deal with disagreements,
and yet many times we do not come close to following this
guidance. Instead, we react in anger, harsh words, gossip, and
strife. In fact, sometimes we treat our brothers and sisters in
Christ worse than we would a stranger.

Let's put into practice what God has said and create
harmony in the church. Knowing we will have disagreements

(on everything from music to the pastor), respond in a way that brings connection where possible and correction when needed. Be an example to the world of a godly community. If you aim for this, you might not hit the mark every time, but you will be heading in the right direction!

Many of us in the church are like porcupines trying to huddle together on a bitter cold night to keep each other warm, but we continually poke and hurt each other the closer we get.

Howard Hendricks

I have never yet known the Spirit of God to work where the Lord's people were divided.

D.L. Moody

Satan greatly approves of our railing at each other, but God does not.

Charles Spurgeon

For Further Reflection
Matthew 18:15–17; Proverbs 17:14; 1 Corinthians 1:10

TODAY'S PRAYER
Lord Jesus, help me be an instrument of your peace in every part of my life. Help me follow your will and, when disagreements come up, to deal with them the way you desire. May I be part of the unity of the church and not division. Amen.

Promise and Oath

So God has given both his promise and his oath.
These two things are unchangeable because it is
impossible for God to lie. Therefore, we who have
fled to him for refuge can have great confidence
as we hold to the hope that lies before us.

HEBREWS 6:18

When our lives are in turmoil and uncertainty swirls, we can lose our focus on the truth. We can get lost in the power of our anger and frustration, trying to create solutions to the challenges we are facing. We get drawn into the drama, which then has our complete attention. In these times, we forget the truth: God is always with us, and nothing that we are experiencing is a mystery to him. He has given both his promise and his oath.

But if God is always with us, why do bad things happen? How could a loving God allow horrible things to happen to us or to our loved ones? We live in a world affected by the ravages of sin, both of our own sin and that of others. Our hope is based on the truth that God promised us power over sin through the resurrection of Christ. God is love, and he has provided a way for us to experience freedom from the ravages of sin. Our earthly existence can be redeemed because of the promise of God's faithfulness.

Knowing that God is trustworthy and that he provides liberty for our souls is comforting. Forgiveness is a gift he gives. Because we are forgiven, we can then forgive what has happened to us. The act of forgiveness frees us from what happened. The past no longer has control. It isn't easy and doesn't always mean reconciliation with the offender. It does mean healing and freedom to move on in our lives. We can be confident in the hope of Christ to heal and redeem our lives. When we put our trust in the promises of God, we have a hope!

With Jesus, even in our darkest moments the best remains, and the very best is yet to be.

Corrie ten Boom

Life is so short. Grudges are a waste of time. Laugh when you can, apologize when you should, and trust God with what you cannot change.

Nicky Gumbel

Forgiving other people who have wronged us or hurt us or embarrassed us is not easy. In fact, sometimes it seems impossible. But that is what God did for us and what he asks us to do for others.

Korie Robertson

For Further Reflection

Proverbs 17:9; Isaiah 43:25; Numbers 14:19-21

TODAY'S PRAYER

Lord God, thank you for your faithfulness! I know I can trust in your promises. Show me where I might be stuck in my own hurt and anger. Give me the power to forgive as you have so graciously forgiven me so that I may be free. Let my life speak of the greatness of You. Amen.

Merciful God

But the Lord our God is merciful and forgiving,
even though we have rebelled against him.

DANIEL 9:9

When you reflect back on your life, do guilt and shame take a grip on your heart? Do you think back on times when your anger caused hurt and pain for someone you love? Our anger used in the wrong way leaves a mark, not only on those we affected but also on us. The good news is you can heal the past through the power of a loving and merciful God.

No matter what you have done, God provides healing and a future free of guilt and shame. The enemy of your soul wants you to believe that what you have done in your past defines you, and that there can be no real change. You must surrender that lie to the truth: God will forgive you! God doesn't look back with judgment. He looks on you as a new creation, because that is what you are.

Your anger might have left a wake of hurt and pain for those you love—and anyone else in your path. When you ask God's forgiveness, you can then ask others to forgive you, and you can make restitution where possible. The pain you caused will be redeemed through the mercy of God. You do not have to be condemned by your past but instead experience freedom from the anger within.

You can be redeemed and free to move into a future where you are whole. You can be in redemptive relationship with others and continue to grow emotionally, mentally, and spiritually. What a great gift from a merciful God!

God creates out of nothing. Wonderful you say. Yes, to be sure, but he does what is still more wonderful: he makes saints out of sinners.

Soren Kierkegaard

God has such gladness every time he sees from heaven that a sinner is praying to him with all his heart, as a mother has when she sees the first smile on her baby's face.

Fyodor Dostoyevsky

Every decision you need to make, every task you need to accomplish, every relationship you need to navigate, every element of daily life you need to traverse, God has already perfectly matched up with an equivalent-to-overflowing supply of His grace.

Priscilla Shirer

For Further Reflection

1 John 4:16; Psalm 90:2; 2 Peter 3:9

TODAY'S PRAYER

Father God, thank you for your mercy and forgiveness. Thank you for the power at work within my heart and relationships. You are an amazing God! Amen.

Day 75

Nearness of God

The Lord is close to the brokenhearted;
he rescues those whose spirits are crushed.

PSALM 34:18

Many people are unaware of how anger is affecting their lives. They seem calm, cool, and collected yet have years of unexpressed frustration and hurt. The anger inside is making an impact spiritually, mentally, emotionally, and physically, and it's affecting personal relationships. Anger can cause us to put up a shield, not letting anyone close enough to cause pain, touch old hurts, or create new wounds.

We all have the potential to carry hurt and anger throughout our lives. We have to be willing to examine anything lingering under the surface that is driving our behaviors. We have to be willing to surrender these wounds to God who knows what we have experienced and can provide healing. Then we will become authentic in our relationships.

Sometimes when we have unresolved anger, we also push away from God. We might wonder why, if God loves me so much, did he allow this wrong? We might think he is not trustworthy or simply not interested in our lives. We begin to believe we are alone and have to figure out life on our own.

God is near, and he is able to deliver us from the lingering effects of the past. Not only that, he is interested in hearing from us. Even though he knows what we are going through, he wants us to express our concerns.

God is as close as our very breath. He will help us heal and live untethered by old wounds. Begin today to let go of the old hurts and trust in God who loves you.

Wide awake to the presence of God, I realized I had been so focused on asking why a good God allowed bad things to happen that I was missing out on the nearness of God all along. In becoming preoccupied with the why, I was missing the who.

Margaret Feinberg

However softly we speak, God is near enough to hear us.

Teresa of Avila

You need not cry very loud; He is nearer to us than we think.

Brother Lawrence

For Further Reflection
John 14:18; James 4:8; Romans 10:11-13

TODAY'S PRAYER
Lord God, help me as I bring my wounds to you. Help me surrender the hurts and frustrations that threaten to take over my life. Reveal the ways that anger has disconnected me from you and others. Create a tender heart in me and renew your spirit within me. Amen.

Day 76

Wise Instruction

Anyone who rebukes a mocker will get an insult in return. Anyone who corrects the wicked will get hurt.

PROVERBS 9:7

Have you ever been in a conversation that started out as a simple sharing of ideas, and then lines were drawn and before you knew it, you were in a full-on argument? Once tempers flare it is difficult to really hear both sides and have a good outcome.

How can you have a healthy discussion where two opposing views are being presented? First, do you listen and hear what the other person is saying, or are you already planning your attack? Be willing to truly listen and consider what the opposing view has to offer.

Second, do you discern your audience? Some people are not interested in hearing what you have to say, which can be frustrating. You might be tempted to correct them, but they might not be the slightest bit interested in another view.

Third, do you approach with the right spirit? Sometimes we struggle with the need to be right or have the last word. An argumentative spirit could come from not feeling heard, either currently or in the past. Perhaps you were overlooked or excluded from previous discussions, and that has created a tension that affects how you talk with others now. They might see you as angry, aggressive, and impatient. You might not be aware of how you come across.

Healthy conversations should be mutual, with appropriate give and take between the people involved. To be a better communicator, remember to listen to others before correcting them; discern where you can offer your opinion and do so with a good spirit; and pay attention to whether anger might be driving your discussion. Following these steps will help you develop new communication strategies and allow you to engage in healthy conversations and discussions.

Great leaders understand that the right attitude will set the right atmosphere, which enables the right response from others.

John Maxwell

Attitudes are more important than facts.

George Macdonald

Further Reflection

James 1:5; Philippians 2:5-11; Ephesians 4:31

TODAY'S PRAYER

Lord Jesus, help me be present in my conversations, not reacting from a place of fear or anger. May I have the patience to hear and the wisdom to know where I can be of help. Help me to be humble and to also know when I need to press into the truth. Amen.

Asking For Help

May God, who gives this patience and encouragement,
help you live in complete harmony with each other,
as is fitting for followers of Christ Jesus.

ROMANS 15:5

Some days seem to go without any effort at all. You wake up on time, you don't forget anything as you leave for the day, and you make all green lights. You feel rested and energized to meet the day. Other days the opposite occurs: You wake up late, forget something important, and hit every stop light. You feel like a weight is on you and have no energy for the day. And you're angry about it.

Maintaining a good attitude is easy when circumstances go well and the people we interact with are pleasant. But when we face obstacle after obstacle, we can become irritated or angry saying, "Why can't anything go my way?" We begin to "share" our day with anyone we encounter, expressing frustration and fury. At this point, basically everyone needs to steer clear!

It's OK to share and ask for support or help. We all have bad days and need to blow off steam in productive and healthy ways. Sharing also helps because people can provide encouragement. It's better to ask for help than stay in the struggle, causing your frustration and stress to boil over.

You can also ask God for help. Sounds simple, yet rarely when we are in the midst of a bad day will we stop and ask for God's help. It's like we reserve prayer for mealtimes and bedtime. Yet God knows what you are experiencing and can provide peace and insight. Prayer will also disrupt the fury long enough to calm your heart rate. Talking to God can help you shift your thoughts and interrupt the frustration so you can take a breath and calm down. When you recognize that God will provide what you need when you need it, you will not hesitate to ask!

God will never cease to help us until we cease to need.

Charles Spurgeon

God knows what each one of us is dealing with. He knows our pressures. He knows our conflicts. And he has made a provision for each and every one of them. That provision is himself in the person of the Holy Spirit, indwelling us and empowering us to respond rightly.

Kay Arthur

For Further Reflection

Psalm 28:7; Colossians 4:2; 1 Thessalonians 5:16–18

TODAY'S PRAYER

Lord Jesus, help me to be aware that you are always there and will provide what I need even before I realize it. Remind me that your presence goes with me every minute of my day. Thank you for all you so graciously provide. Amen.

Bite Your Tongue

Indeed, we all make many mistakes. For if we could control our tongues, we would be perfect and could also control ourselves in every other way.

JAMES 3:2

How many times do our mouths engage before our brains? We say things in the heat of the moment and regret those words as soon as they leave our lips. If only we could take back what we say in anger.

Can anyone ever control what they say when they are angry? Yes, but not in the heat of the moment. Gaining control of our tongues requires a change of heart and mind, and it demands daily practice. Many times we say, "I can't help it; it just comes out." The truth is, it comes out because it's inside our hearts and minds. We need self-control to prevent our tongues from wreaking havoc. We must learn a new language—one that isn't reactive and vindictive.

Changing how we speak is a work of God in our lives. As we grow in faith, we learn how to live in a way that reflects him in all we do. Then we must practice the new way of life every day until it becomes our nature. Changing our speech will be challenging at first, and we will have slip-ups along the way, but one day we will gain greater control over our tongues, using words to express feelings without causing pain to others.

Begin today by reflecting on how you use your words when you are angry. Have you gotten into the habit of using sarcasm or criticism, or being unkind in how you speak? The first step of change is awareness of what needs to change. Examine the way you express yourself and ask God to reveal what part of your speech needs to go. Eventually you'll be surprised, in a good way, of what comes out of your mouth.

———————▲———————

Patience is the ability to idle your motor when you feel like stripping your gears.

Barbara Johnson

Growth takes time. God knows that. I know that. And to my surprise, his abundance is mine in the process—not as a prize at the end.

Carol Kent

God does not always heal us instantly the way we think. He is not a jack-in-the-box God. But God is walking with me through this.

Thelma Wells

———————▲———————

For Further Reflection

Psalm 141:3; Galatians 6:1; Proverbs 10:19

TODAY'S PRAYER

Lord Jesus, I want to reflect you in all that I say—even in times of anger. Put a guard over my mouth and clean my heart and mind of anything that doesn't reflect you. Thank you for your loving kindness and faithfulness to me. Amen.

Day 79

Maturity

Dear brothers and sisters, I close my letter with these
last words: Be joyful. Grow to maturity. Encourage
each other. Live in harmony and peace. Then the
God of love and peace will be with you.

2 Corinthians 13:11

Is life going the way you hoped? As children, we imagine
how exciting and wonderful life will be when we grow up.
When we reach adulthood, we find out life isn't as easy as
we dreamed. Have you encountered obstacles along the way
that you just can't move? Have your disappointments and
hurts, maybe even failures, created a wound? Are you angry
because things didn't turn out the way you expected?

If anything has caused you to stall in your life and anger has
been your response, it's time to grow up. That sounds harsh, but
it's the truth. Growing up will require some hard, healing work
and a willingness to confront the anger and disappointment
inside. When you were younger, you might have believed that if
you did all the right things, life would be a dream. Life doesn't
work that way. If you can accept the realities of your life, you
will be able to heal and move toward a better future.

Growing in maturity will be a lifelong process that requires
God's help. The way you react to life has to change, and you
will need help in learning a new way to respond to life. If you
can easily identify the source of your wound, begin there. You
might need to work with a counselor, go to a grief group or a
recovery group, and begin to process what has caused anger

and hurt in your life. You can begin a healing journey that will offer peace, joy, and a new future.

Don't stay stuck. You can overcome and thrive in your life. It will take some time and help but it will be worth every minute. Begin today!

The marvelous richness of human experience would lose something of rewarding joy if there were no limitations to overcome. The hilltop hour would not be half so wonderful if there were no dark valleys to traverse.

Helen Keller

All the adversity I've had in my life, all my troubles and obstacles, have strengthened me…. You may not realize it when it happens, but a kick in the teeth may be the best thing in the world for you.

Walt Disney

The most beautiful people I've known are those who have known trials, have known struggles, have known loss, and have found their way out of the depths.

Elisabeth Kübler-Ross

For Further Reflection
James 1:2-4; Psalm 46:1; Philippians 4:13

TODAY'S PRAYER
Lord Jesus, you know the wounds I have from my journey. I ask you to heal my hurts so that I can mature in my faith and in my life. You are the source of my strength and healing. Amen.

For the Good

And we know that God causes everything to work together for the good of those who love God and are called according to his purpose for them.

Romans 8:28

When you face difficulties or tragedies, anger might flare at the unfairness of the situation. An unexpected diagnosis, betrayal, or devastating event can create feelings of rage and fury. You struggle to make sense of what happened, thinking it's impossible to see how anything good can come from it. Well-meaning people might offer this passage of scripture as a way to bring some comfort. But when you are that upset, you don't want to hear that what's happened is all for the good.

Allowing yourself to express your feelings is important. At traumatic times in our lives, we will have a full range of emotions, including shock, sadness, anger, and frustration. Some of these feelings will be big in the moment but will lessen with time. Others will remain and, if there is no resolution, grow as time goes on. The way through these challenges is difficult, gut wrenching, and life altering. Allowing yourself to express those feelings can make a huge difference in your future self.

The anger you feel when the unexpected occurs is understandable. But God is at work in your situation. The "good" that this passage refers to isn't that everything will come together with a nice, neat bow on top. Sometimes the good won't make sense this side of heaven. Trust that God will work everything out eventually. Allow the feelings to come, release the anger and the sadness, and allow God to provide peace for you regardless of the outcome of the situation. Healing might take longer than you ever imagined, but trusting that God is with you and will work in the details will help as you go through this difficult journey.

When suffering is sharp and profound, I expect and believe that God will meet me in its midst. But in the struggles of my average day I somehow feel I have a right to be annoyed.

Tish Harrison Warren

What was intended to harm, God intended it all for good. And no matter what intends to harm you, God's arms have you. You can never be undone.

Ann Voskamp

Pain and trials are almost constant companions, but never enemies. They drive me into his sovereign arms. There he takes my disappointments and works everything together for good.

Kay Arthur

For Further Reflection

James 1:12; Psalm 16:8; Proverbs 17:14

TODAY'S PRAYER

Lord Jesus, I do not understand why I am going through this trouble. However, I will choose to trust that you are working in the mess and that you will heal my heart. I pray for your help. Amen.

Unity

A kingdom divided by civil war will collapse. Similarly,
a family splintered by feuding will fall apart.

MARK 3:24–25

Family fights have been around since the beginning of time: Cain and Abel, Jacob and Esau, Rachel and Leah, and the list goes on. Why is it so hard for families to get along?

Disagreements are inevitable; family members have different opinions because of their differing perspectives. And no one is perfect—we all struggle with sin and self-centeredness. When facing an argument, we must resist reacting in anger and creating a rift. This can be especially difficult when a family member is in the wrong or trying to incite division.

Families will not agree on everything, but if arguing and fighting become the norm, eventually relationships will dissolve. The first step toward avoiding division is to recognize the value of unity and work toward that. Pursuing unity doesn't mean opinions aren't welcome; rather, it is respecting opinions, listening to each other, and deciding together to work toward what is best for the whole.

You might try to listen, respect, and offer to talk about issues, but the other person might not be willing to do the same. This can be painful and frustrating. If the other person isn't interested in preserving the relationship, there isn't much you can do. It is important, however, not to fan the flames of the disagreement. Work on grieving the loss, pray for peace, and pray for the family member(s) who broke the relationship. Have an attitude of forgiveness similar to what Joseph experienced when his family returned after leaving him for dead; in Genesis 50:20 Joseph says, "You intended to harm me, but God intended it all for good." Allow God to work in your life despite the family discord, knowing that God can work through all the challenges we face.

Train up a child in the way he should go—but be sure you go that way yourself.

Charles Spurgeon

What can you do to promote world peace? Go home and love your family.

Mother Teresa

All happy families are alike; each unhappy family is unhappy in its own way.

Leo Tolstoy

For Further Reflection

1 Corinthians 1:10; Philippians 2:3–4; Luke 6:27–31

TODAY'S PRAYER

Lord Jesus, you have placed me in my family and you know the challenges within. Help me to be humble, respectful, and listen well. When family ties are threatened, help me to reach out and connect. Help me discern where I need to ask forgiveness or offer forgiveness. Amen.

Hot vs. Cool

A hot-tempered person starts fights;
a cool-tempered person stops them.

PROVERBS 15:18

Would you describe your temperament as hot or cool? You probably know right away where you usually land, and if you are unsure ask someone who is close to you how they would describe your personality.

Proverbs 15:18 is straightforward: someone who is hot-tempered starts fights. You might be this person. You feel as though the world needs to be set straight on so many things, and people just can't get things right. Every discussion turns into a battle to win, and relationships tend to be tentative, with the other person trying not to upset you. You probably have high blood pressure and tension headaches.

Imagine what it would feel like to not be subject to your temperament but instead be self-controlled and cool-tempered. You would not be reactive to every problem you encounter; rather, you would give a measured response. You would be a person who is able to discuss challenging issues without blowing up. With a cool temperament, you could use wisdom and discernment to deal with difficulties because your brain would work better. Your thoughts would not get as easily hijacked by emotion.

If you have been in the hot-tempered category for any length of time, you will have some work to do to turn down the temperature, and it will likely be one degree at a time. The good news is that you are able to change. You can begin today to work toward becoming a person who is responsive, flexible, and cool-tempered.

As long as I viewed someone as the enemy, I gave that person some power over my life. But as I forgave a person, I too was free.

Sheila Walsh

It's so important to realize that every time you get upset, it drains your emotional energy. Losing your cool makes you tired. Getting angry a lot messes with your health.

Joyce Meyer

Self-aware people understand not only what their own emotions and actions are but also how their emotions and actions affect others.

Carey Nieuwhof

For Further Reflections

Romans 12:1–2; 2 Corinthians 5:17; Ezekiel 36:26

TODAY'S PRAYER

Heavenly Father, please help me as I seek to adjust the temperature of my attitude. Help me to slow down my reactions, quicken my ability to hear others, and wait upon you for direction. Help me to become more like you every day. Amen.

Simple Instructions

Do everything without complaining and arguing, so that
no one can criticize you. Live clean, innocent lives
as children of God, shining like bright lights in
a world full of crooked and perverse people.

PHILIPPIANS 2:14–15

What things bug you? Maybe people being late infuriates you. Maybe you cannot understand why restaurants can't train their staff correctly, and a night out for dinner becomes a battleground. Maybe people don't listen to you, which makes you angry. If these scenarios sound familiar, you might need a makeover.

We all require constant remodeling—sometimes even a complete renovation. As believers, the Holy Spirit is active in our lives, sanctifying us each day to conform us more to the image of Christ. Often we have difficulty addressing our own issues, instead focusing on what others should be doing differently or complaining that things in general are all wrong. Constant complaining, arguing, and irritability indicate we are in need of help.

A makeover requires demolition to tear down walls we have built—walls like criticism, contempt, judgment, impatience, and anger. Then we have to examine what is behind these walls, hidden issues that have been creating a life that doesn't resemble the life Jesus died for us to have. Behind the walls we often find deep hurt, pain, and sadness. When we give these things to Christ, he will provide a way to rebuild on a foundation of love, grace, and truth. The Holy Spirit, our craftsman, will begin to re-fashion our attitudes from anger, irritation, and self-righteousness to self-control, patience, peace, and joy.

Philippians 2:14 provides an inspection checklist for our new outlook, and the first item on the list is: "Do everything without complaining and arguing." *Everything.* The instruction is simple, yet try to follow this for one day and you will discover how much work you have to do. The good news is that you are not on your own in this process. God will lead you in the best reconstruction project ever.

It's been said that we are shaped by our thoughts. If this is true, can you imagine where one healthy thought can lead each day?

Christine Caine

I'm living my life for an audience of one. I live my life to please God.

Anne Graham Lotz

For Further Reflection
Colossians 3:5–10; Galatians 2:20; Psalm 1:1–3

TODAY'S PRAYER
Lord Jesus, you know the walls I have built and where I need major remodeling in my life. I surrender my plans to you so that I can build a life that reflects your glory. Thank you for continuing to work on me. Amen.

Fighting Well

*Be strong and courageous! Do not be afraid
or discouraged. For the Lord your God
is with you wherever you go.*

JOSHUA 1:9

Injustice, victimization, betrayal, and broken trust make us angry. We can carry anger inside and it can affect different parts of our lives. Unresolved anger can actually make us sick physically. We can feel like we are in the fight of our lives, defending the hurt places in our past. Triggered by trauma, we are ready for the battle and not always understanding the war within.

God has provided a way of healing from the past. No matter what we have experienced, God can and will restore us with help from his word, prayer, and trusted people who will walk alongside us in the journey. When we don't realize what our past is doing to our present, we continue to suffer the effects. Trauma needs healing. Anger is just one of many emotional reactions we will experience as a result of old wounds. God has a new life for us to experience.

The process of healing will take time and proper help and support. But fighting for healing and wholeness is vital. Hold tightly to the truth that God loves you, can restore you, and can provide healing for your heart. God's grace and mercy will supply what you will need. One day at a time, press toward the goal of a life free of the pain of the past.

Believers are never told to become one; we already are one and are expected to act like it.

Joni Eareckson Tada

Remember, no matter what your battle is, it is not yours; the battle belongs to the Lord, and He has a plan to bring you victory.

Joyce Meyer

Happiness is dependent on self-discipline. We are the biggest obstacles to our own happiness. It is much easier to do battle with society and with others than to fight our own nature.

Dennis Prager

For Further Reflection

2 Corinthians 10:3-4; Philippians 2:2;
1 Corinthians 15:57

TODAY'S PRAYER

Lord God, you are able to heal and restore my hurting heart, my angry heart, my broken heart. Knowing that you are with me and will supply what I need gives me confidence to take the next step toward healing. I entrust you with these tender places knowing you will make all things right in your time. Amen.

A New Creation

*This means that anyone who belongs to Christ
has become a new person. The old life is gone;
a new life has begun!*

2 Corinthians 5:17

The hardest part about making a change in life—whether it be to lose weight, get a better job, or improve a relationship—is taking the first step. Deciding to deal with unaddressed anger can feel overwhelming. The core wound where the anger began needs healing before the ripple effects can change. Healing work is painful, but anger is like a cancer that will spread if not cut out. Anger is not wrong. Buried anger is lethal.

When we do healing and recovery work, reflecting on what caused the anger can trigger intense emotional responses as we revisit the trauma. Professional help in this process can be extremely helpful. As details of the trauma surface and we express anger and rage, we need a supportive person or team. It is possible to heal the wound, forgive what happened, and not allow anger and its effects continue to rule our lives.

As we move forward in recovery, we will continue to make changes. Sometimes anger has such a strong hold, it can feel like we will never have it under control. However, it is possible to experience a new life, one that has a peace that overcomes the past and is connected with redemptive relationships. The new life doesn't resemble the old life at all! Now we will access anger and process it in a healthy way, experiencing a new life of self-control.

When we surrender to Jesus and let him direct our path, we experience a life of freedom. If you are a follower of Christ but are having trouble with anger, surrender that anger—and the wound that started it—to the love and care of Jesus and experience a new joy, peace, and freedom in your life.

True Christlikeness, true companionship with Christ, comes at the point where it is hard not to respond as he would.

Dallas Willard

No step taken in faith is wasted, not by a God who makes all things new.

Rachel Held Evans

You haven't been through one thing that God cannot heal you from.

Beth Moore

For Further Reflection

Romans 12:1-2; Philippians 4:8-9; Galatians 2:20

TODAY'S PRAYER

Thank you, Lord, for a new life! Your faithfulness to me is overwhelming. Your love and care for me is immeasurable. I know you are with me and will direct my life. Help me to bring you glory in my life. Amen.

Day 86

Seeking God

In my desperation I prayed, and the Lord listened;
he saved me from all my troubles.

<small>PSALM 34:6</small>

When we're in a situation that makes us so angry we can hardly see straight, it's difficult to seek God—especially if we're mad at him. We tend to seek control first. Anger has alerted us to a threat or wrongdoing. Our center of attention narrows and we zoom in on how to fix the problem.

Such focus in itself is not wrong; however, it can sometimes make situations worse. When we hit this point, our rational brain is not calling the shots; our emotional brain is. We make poor decisions when we're enraged. A high level of emotion, in this case anger, indicates we need to pause before reacting. But in that moment, pausing is counterintuitive—our alarm system is going off, and it is difficult to ignore. But we need to put some space between the event and our response, and in this space, we have to seek God for peace, self-control, and direction.

How can we seek God when we're fueled by emotion? By practicing. First, recognize that the response is reactive. Second, at the initial signs of anger—tension, increased blood pressure, clenched teeth—take a second or two and breathe. Nothing will be resolved in those early moments when we'd typically react. Third, pray for clarity, composure, and direction.

The last part of Psalm 34:6 is our hope: "he saved me from all my troubles." This verse doesn't mean we won't have a cause for anger again; rather, when we are angry, our reaction doesn't have to worsen the situation. When we seek God first, he will save us from our troubles by guiding us along the right path, toward a good end.

Prayer enables you to tap into God's wisdom anywhere, anytime, no matter what's going on.

Elizabeth George

People look at me and see a calm, cool guy on the sidelines and I want them to know that my Christian faith affects my coaching and everything I do.

Tony Dungy

Don't let the hurt of today blind you to the hope of tomorrow. Disappointment ushers in a new appointment.

Lysa TerKeurst

For Further Reflection

Isaiah 55:6–9; Proverbs 8:17; 1 Chronicles 16:11

TODAY'S PRAYER

Lord, help me seek you first before I react. Help me trust you to provide wisdom for my challenges, direction for the problems I face, and the peace to trust you in the process. Help me lean on your truth. Thank you for your ever-present love. Amen.

Day 87

Plot Twist

*This change of plans greatly upset Jonah,
and he became very angry.*

JONAH 4:1

Many circumstances can trigger anger. Betrayal, threat, and injustice are among them, and they're legitimate causes for anger. Sometimes something as simple as a change in plans can create anger. A traffic jam that forces us to find a new route frustrates us with its delay. We might have been looking forward to a special event when something—perhaps a pandemic—cancels everything. Being upset and even angry is understandable.

Anger can keep us from thinking clearly. We might get so invested in how we think things are supposed to go that we cannot manage our emotional response when our expectations are not met. Reactions that are bigger than the change of circumstance justifies can indicate there is more to the problem than what is on the surface. A disproportionate reaction is like a warning light on the dashboard telling us to look beneath the surface. What causes the short fuse and the big reaction? We might think it is the current issue, but that might have simply scratched off the scab of an unhealed wound.

If your anger at unanticipated changes in life overtakes you and your reactions become part of the problem, you are more rigid than flexible, and your inability to consider new options compounds the situation. Flexibility is key to dealing with the changes you will experience in life. Recognizing that life will have many plot twists along the way will create some flex in your thinking and planning.

Decide today to increase your flexibility and to reduce your reactions to the plot twist you will experience. Look for how God will work in your life even in the unexpected places.

------------◆------------

The greater part of our happiness or misery depends upon our dispositions, and not upon our circumstances.

Martha Washington

When you are no longer able to change a situation, you are challenged to change yourself. And that changes everything.

Marc Chernoff

Blessed are the flexible, for they shall not be bent out of shape.

Michael McGriffy

------------◆------------

For Further Reflection
Luke 11:9–10; Hosea 10:12; Romans 8:28

TODAY'S PRAYER
Lord Jesus, increase my trust in you. Remind me that you are working even in the upsets I experience in my life. Help my reactions to reflect you. Help me to know that what you are doing will not be disrupted by what I think are unexpected interruptions. Amen.

God's Revenge

Dear friends, never take revenge. Leave that to the righteous anger of God. For the Scriptures say, "I will take revenge; I will pay them back," says the Lord.

ROMANS 12:19

Anger can cause us to want to take revenge on those who have wronged us. Many people would likely cheer us on as we plot payback against those who caused us pain. We can ruminate about what we could do and how good it would feel to meet out retribution. The problem with this thinking is it just isn't God's way.

Waiting on God to right the wrong might feel like a lifetime, and in some cases we might not know how God handles the wrongdoing until heaven. Waiting means surrendering the outcome to God, completely trusting that he will make all things right in his time. To trust God in this way is a choice we make, and one we might have to make it every day.

Not taking vengeance on someone doesn't mean letting people take advantage. We should report any crime to the authorities. We might have to set boundaries to decrease interacting with the offender. We might need to share with a trusted person the extent of what happened to us, and our anger about the situation. And we will have to rest in the fact that, after we have taken appropriate action, we must trust God to make all things right.

When we make these choices, we will experience the grace and peace of God for each day. We will no longer be driven by resentment, bitterness and a drive for revenge. Instead, we will release the pain of the anger, grieve the losses, and surrender the outcome to God's way of resolving the matter. Living life in this way is really the best revenge—the offender no longer has hold on us. We are free to experience healing.

The best revenge is to be unlike him who performed the injury.

Marcus Aurelius

Revenge and retaliation always perpetuate the cycle of anger, fear, and violence.

Coretta Scott King

Revenge is a confession of pain.

Latin Proverb

For Further Reflection

Psalm 7:11; Romans 1:18; 1 Peter 3:9

TODAY'S PRAYER

Lord you know that I want to pay back those who hurt me. However, I am ready to surrender to your will and your way, knowing that as I trust in you that you will heal me and provide peace for my journey. Amen.

Staying Healthy

Surely resentment destroys the fool,
and jealousy kills the simple.

Certain traits of anger, if allowed to persist, will cause the death of relationships and destroy the ability to connect with others. A few of these aspects of anger are resentment, jealousy, bitterness, violence, bullying, and harassment. These come from anger somewhere inside, and if we are unable to recognize the source and root it out, we will suffer the harm from the effects.

When anger triggers resentment, we can close off ourselves to life. Resentment could mean we don't like when other people succeed, or it could manifest as secretly hating someone for what they have done to us. Either way, resentment is a surefire way to kill connections that are important in life.

Do you recognize resentment in your life? Resentment has to be addressed and resolved, and the way to do this is to forgive the person or let go of the situation. Release the grip that resentment has on you, because it can kill your ability to connect with other people—people you love and care for— who *haven't* caused you pain.

Job 5:2 also addresses the aspect of jealousy, an intense desire to have what someone else has. You might be angry that they have what you want, and you begin to obsess over how unfair it is or how to get back at them. Such a waste of energy!

Instead, be grateful for what you have. Focus on the blessings in your life and you will be released from the grip of jealousy.

All of the aspects of anger threaten your life and wellbeing. God wants us to be free of the things that want to claim our life. We have to surrender the places that we have been hurt—where we feel insecure, threatened, and wronged—to God who is able to heal our hearts.

When the root is bitterness, imagine what the fruit might be.

Woodrow Kroll

Resentment always hurts you more than the person you resent.

Rick Warren

O, Jealousy, thou ugliest fiend of hell! Thy deadly venom preys on my vitals, turns the healthful hue of my fresh cheek to haggard shallowness, and drinks my spirit up.

Hannah More

For Further Reflection

Proverbs 23:17-18; James 3:14-16; Psalm 37:1-3

TODAY'S PRAYER

Lord Jesus, thank you for your ability to heal me from the inside out. Search me and show me where resentment, jealousy, or any anger is within me. I want to be free to live my life in the way you intended. Amen.

Day 90

God's Way

*The Lord is slow to get angry, but his power is great,
and he never lets the guilty go unpunished. He
displays his power in the whirlwind and the storm.
The billowing clouds are the dust beneath his feet.*

Nahum 1:3

The human condition is such that we desire to be in control. We exert this power where we can, and when it is thwarted, we often feel frustrated and angry. We want things the way we want them when we want them. However, our Creator is the one who is truly in control, though he gives us the freedom to make choices.

God wants us to follow his ways, maturing in our faith and trust in him. We can trust God to deal with the difficulties and hardships in our lives. When things don't go our way, we don't need to react irrationally, trying to exert our power. Instead we can trust that God sees our difficulty and will make things right. He is slow to get angry—which is a pattern we can adopt. His power is great. We do not have to help him make things right. Instead we can remind ourselves God is in control.

Slowing our anger means we are not reacting using our power to try to fix the wrong. Being slow to anger does not mean we have to sit by and do nothing. Instead, we recognize what we can do and express our feelings in a respectful way that attacks the problem not the person. We can pray, asking God to reveal what he wants from us. And we can trust that God will redeem the situation.

It can comfort us to know that even when we don't feel like God is working in our situation, he absolutely is! Trust in God's power to work in all of your life knowing he is able.

Suffering may be someone's fault or it may not be anyone's fault. But if given to God, our suffering becomes an opportunity to experience the power of God at work in our lives and to give glory to him.

Anne Graham Lotz

Assurance grows by repeated conflict, by our repeated experimental proof of the Lord's power and goodness to save; when we have been brought very low and helped, sorely wounded and healed, cast down and raised again, have given up all hope, and been suddenly snatched from danger, and placed in safety; and when these things have been repeated to us and in us a thousand times over, we begin to learn to trust simply to the word and power of God, beyond and against appearances: and this trust, when habitual and strong, bears the name of assurance; for even assurance has degrees.

John Newton

For Further Reflection
Isaiah 26:4; Exodus 14:14; 2 Peter 1:3

TODAY'S PRAYER
Lord, your way is the best. Help me to follow you instead of trying to control everything. As I trust you I can know and continue to experience your power at work in my life. You are the Almighty God! There is not one greater than you! Amen.

Day 91

Release It

But as I stood there in silence—not even speaking
of good things—the turmoil within me grew worse.

Psalm 39:2

Counseling is a great resource when you are struggling with emotional and mental issues. Yet it can be difficult to ask for help. Maybe that you think you should be able to deal with your struggles on your own. You might think counseling is for other people, not you. Maybe the pain you are experiencing is so deep inside that you don't even know what life would be like without it. You might even think counseling won't do any good because you can't change the past. These reasons are actually just excuses for seeking help.

Too often we suffer needlessly, not knowing that help is available. The pain we experience then becomes the pain we carry, which in turn changes who we are. Our unresolved pain and hurt affects every aspect of our life.

People who go to counseling begin to understand things about themselves that provide insight into a better life experience. Counseling doesn't change a person's past but can help them talk it out and release the pain inside. Christian counselors also use the word of God to help people understand how their faith will make a difference in their healing and recovery. Sometimes the issues are about our faith. Counseling helps release what is inside to help us experience a healthy life.

Perhaps you have thought about going to a counselor but are unsure. Research what a counseling session is like, what therapy can help you with, and maybe look for a therapist near you. You could talk with them on the phone about what kind of issues they work with, if they are a Christian counselor, and what payment options are. Sometimes these simple steps help decrease resistance. If you have been struggling, help is available. You are worth being cared for.

Anger may be handled wrongly in either one of two ways: blowing up and clamming up.

Jay Adams

Anything that's human is mentionable, and anything that is mentionable can be more manageable.

Fred Rogers

Further Reflection

Proverbs 12:15; Ephesians 4:22–24; 1 Peter 5:7

TODAY'S PRAYER

Lord Jesus, help me ask for help. Knowing that I may be resistant, change my heart. I want to live in the way you have planned for me, not in a reclusive, wounded state. Please direct me to the right help and provide a place where healing can begin. Thank you in advance for your loving care of me. Amen.

Godly Behavior

But the wisdom from above is first of all pure. It is also peace loving, gentle at all times, and willing to yield to others. It is full of mercy and the fruit of good deeds. It shows no favoritism and is always sincere.

JAMES 3:17

Anger and the behaviors that accompany it are something we have to learn to control. It isn't something we should ignore, stuff, or repress—that is unhealthy. Rather, when we work on controlling our anger and our behavior, we can behave in a way that will produce something good, rather than react in a way that will bring more problems.

When we are following God's way, our life changes for the good. Our old ways of dealing with the troubles and strife of this world should not be part of our new life. James 3:17 begins with "the wisdom from above is first of all pure." When we accept Christ and follow him, our hearts are purified. As we yield our lives, our attitudes, actions, and behaviors will also change, and we will become peace loving, gentle, humble, and full of mercy.

We will still experience anger, fear, frustration, sadness, and many other emotions. But the behaviors that accompany these normal human emotions will be self-controlled, which is a fruit of the Spirit. Our responses when we're angry will not be out of control, causing more hurt to others. Self-control might sound impossible but it can be realized.

Begin to surrender your life fully to the ways of God. There will always be things in life that will challenge you. God can help you live through the most difficult times with grace and a full range of emotions that will reflect the new person you are in Christ. Transformation is possible.

Spiritual transformation into Christlikeness in not going to happen unless we act... What transforms us is the will to obey Jesus Christ.

Dallas Willard

He is intangible and invisible. But his work is more powerful than the most ferocious wind. The Spirit brings order out of chaos and beauty out of ugliness. He can transform a sin-blistered man into a paragon of virtue. The Spirit changes people. The Author of life is also the Transformer of life.

R.C. Sproul

We need never shout across the spaces to an absent God. He is nearer than our own soul, closer than our most secret thoughts.

A.W. Tozer

For Further Reflections
2 Corinthians 3:18; Psalm 51:10-12; Colossians 1:10

TODAY'S PRAYER
Lord Jesus, create in me a clean heart, mind, and behavior. I want to follow your leading. Help me as I begin surrender my life completely to you. I trust that you know the best way for me, and I am willing. I ask this in the power of your name. Amen.

Day 93

Steadfast

*He lifted me out of the pit of despair, out of the mud
and the mire. He set my feet on solid ground
and steadied me as I walked along.*

PSALM 40:2

When we feel upset and angry, our mood, appetite, reasoning, and even our physical body experiences the effects. After the initial rage has run its course, we can start to feel stuck, that nothing can be done to change what has happened. Anger literally becomes like a pit, and we can live there a long time, actually getting comfortable in the discomfort.

Some people never escape because they don't recognize they're stuck. How can you tell if you are stuck in such anger? Ask yourself a couple of questions: Are you ruminating over what happened? Are you telling the story to anyone who will listen—and even those who won't? Are you more angry than when it first occurred? These are signs you might be in a pit.

Getting out of the pit will require God's help, which will include other people, prayer, forgiveness, and acceptance. You will need trusted people who can support you as you process your anger—people willing to listen but not join you in the pit; after all, if they end up in the pit they cannot help you out. Prayer helps you access God's healing power and strength as you begin the climb out of the pit. Forgiveness enables you to move on and let go of the debt your offender owes you. Acceptance indicates you have moved out of the pit.

These steps are not neat and tidy, and some may take longer than you imagined. You might have difficulty praying, but commit to opening up your heart to God. When you are struggling, ask your trusted people to pray for you. God is faithful to lift you out of your pit and set you on solid ground.

I may walk with a spiritual limp, but thanks be to God, who holds me up and urges me to lean on him, at least I can walk. So can you. Walk away from that pit before it's the death of you.

Beth Moore

God is constantly on the move. I cannot stay where I am and follow God at the same time; responding requires movement.

Margaret Feinberg

God is able to take the mess of our past and turn it into a message. He takes the trials and tests and turns them into a testimony.

Christine Caine

For Further Reflection

Romans 12:12; Jeremiah 17:14; Galatians 5:1

TODAY'S PRAYER

Lord God, help me out of this pit. Lead me to where you want me to go. Forgive my lack of trust that you will make all things right in your time. Heal my wounds and create in me a whole heart that wants all you have for me. Amen.

Be Bold

People who wink at wrong cause trouble,
but a bold reproof promotes peace.

PROVERBS 10:10

Sometimes we are so committed to keeping the peace we do not address obvious problems. We don't speak up when we feel we have been mistreated or cheated. When we are offended, we stuff the feeling and move on, instead of saying anything to correct the issue. Sometimes we pack down our anger until it becomes too much, and the lid blows off. How do we control our anger and avoid extremes?

If you tend to be the type of person who overlooks an offense, that can be good. The problem is when you overlook an offense that needs to be confronted. A bold reproof, as this Proverb says, promotes peace. But you might be hesitant, thinking the situation will just get worse if you confront the issue. Yes, addressing the problem might make the conversation heated, but you might also be able to press through to an understanding that could make a positive difference.

Being bold doesn't have to mean being loud and harsh; rather, it's being confident and strong, making a move. Boldness can help settle a dispute without attacking the other person. So many people will dismiss things that are not OK in a relationship to avoid disturbing the peace when the better choice would be to speak up.

You might feel angry and don't know how to express it in a way that will bring about peace or understanding. Ask for help if you need to make a bold move to correct a wrong. Remember, your anger is a signal that something is wrong. Pay attention and then work through a solution. This is a necessary part of any relationship.

———————▲———————

Past boldness is no assurance of future boldness. Boldness demands continual reliance on God's spirit.

Andy Stanley

Boldness in the course of a noble fight is worth the risk... If you stand on truth, you'll only regret your timidity later, but you'll never regret being bold.

Charles R. Swindoll

Boldness is behavior born out of belief.

Craig Groeschel

———————▲———————

For Further Reflection

2 Timothy 1:7; Deuteronomy 31:8; Psalm 50:15

TODAY'S PRAYER

Heavenly Father, help me to be bold when there is cause. I pray for your wisdom and strength when there is wrong to be confronted. I pray for self-control and grace as I speak. Make me more like you, for your glory. Amen.

Spirit-Filled Life

*Since we are living by the Spirit, let us follow
the Spirit's leading in every part of our lives.*

GALATIANS 5:25

The Holy Spirit plays a vital part in the life of a follower of Jesus Christ. As we grow in our faith, the Holy Spirit heals us, teaches us, leads us to a better understanding of scripture, and intercedes for us in prayer. The Holy Spirit is a gift and a powerful force in our lives. What does this have to do with anger?

In Galatians 5, the apostle Paul talks about how living a spirit-filled life will transform our thoughts and actions. In verse 20, Paul lists "outbursts of anger" as an example of living by the sinful nature. In contrast, when we are letting the Holy Spirit guide us, we are sensitive to his prompting toward godly responses. There is less room for our old nature and more evidence of the new life in us.

Think about it this way: If you are having outbursts of anger, does that resemble Jesus or you? If you are able to control your temper, does that resemble Jesus or you? The godly changes in your life, including self-control, are the fruit of the spirit working in you. As you seek the Lord through the word, through prayer, and through connecting with other believers, your life will reflect less of our old, sinful nature and more of the new nature Christ has given you. It really is an amazing gift!

Take a few moments today and read the fifth chapter of Galatians. When you look at the lists of behaviors and attitudes, take a personal inventory. Which of these describe your life more accurately? Ask the Lord to reveal where you need to change. Invite the Holy Spirit to work in your life and experience the freedom Christ died for you to have!

The first secret to loving others is to immerse yourself in a love relationship with God the Father, God the Son, and God the Holy Spirit—and abide there.

Anne Graham Lotz

The Holy Spirit wants to convert the words of Scripture into transformed personalities.

David Jeremiah

The Holy Spirit gives liberty to the Christian, direction to the worker, discernment to the teacher, power to the Word, and fruit to faithful service. He reveals the things of Christ.

Billy Graham

For Further Reflection

Ezekiel 36:27; 2 Corinthians 3:17; John 14:16

TODAY'S PRAYER

Lord Jesus, thank you for the precious gift of your Holy Spirit! I pray for this power to move in me and transform my life to your likeness. May the fruit of the Spirit be evident in my life. I want to live in the freedom you have given me. Amen.

Day 96

Love, Not Hate

Hatred stirs up quarrels, but love makes up for all offenses.

Proverbs 10:12

Relationships are a vital part of life, but with interpersonal relationships come good and bad experiences. God created us for connection, and yet many times the connections we make can be the most challenging part of our lives.

When we are hurt in a relationship, we tend to become angry over the wrong done to us, which is a normal response. Following that, we can either stay angry—perhaps even to the point of hating the person—or work through the problem. Unfortunately, when the offense is deeply hurtful, we have a hard time seeing anything other than hate and anger. It literally stirs us up. When anger darkens to hatred in our hearts, we are in a dangerous place. Hatred must be uprooted and eliminated. When hate is inside us, we focus on retaliation or revenge. God wants to bring forgiveness and restoration—wholeness—to our lives.

When we can work through the issue and forgive, our hearts can be whole again. Although some relationships cannot be reconciled, when we forgive, the part of us that was wounded will love again. Love is a powerful force and can make up for offenses. Love doesn't approve wrongdoing or allow people to hurt us. But when we can love and not hate, life is full and free.

If you recognize that you need to increase your love, don't wait another minute. Forgive the offense and begin to work on your healing. Decide to not allow hate to have any place in your heart. Making this change might take time, but it might also save your life. Love is the answer.

We must develop and maintain the capacity to forgive. He who is devoid of the power to forgive is devoid of the power to love. There is some good in the worst of us and some evil in the best of us. When we discover this, we are less prone to hate our enemies.

Martin Luther King, Jr.

Lord, make me an instrument of thy peace. Where there is hatred, let me sow love.

Francis of Assisi

I also think it's hard to hate one person but love another. It's hard to treat anybody right when our heart isn't right. Even people you want to love may be suffering from your bitterness, resentment, and unforgiveness.

Joyce Meyer

For Further Reflection

1 John 4:19-20; Leviticus 19:17-18; Hebrews 12:15

TODAY'S PRAYER

Lord Jesus, please help me heal the wounds of my heart and to keep hate from entering in. I want to love like you and have redemptive relationships. Help me to forgive and to let go of any bitterness or anger that is in my heart. Amen.

All Grown Up

A truly wise person uses few words; a person
with understanding is even-tempered.

PROVERBS 17:27

f you have been around a toddler, you know how powerful they can be—not their strength but their temper! Toddlers have quick tempers, and when they don't like something, they let everyone know. They'll throw themselves on the ground no matter where they are—home, church, a store—any place the anger strikes.

This stage of life can last a long time, maybe even a lifetime, if we don't learn to master powerful feelings. Do you recognize aspects of your toddler past in your adult anger? Is it difficult for you to keep a restraint on the anger? Are you given to fits? The adult version of fits would be throwing things, punching things, slamming doors, etc. These actions can feel like a release, but if they are destructive, they just make situations worse.

We need to grow up in our emotions. What served us as toddlers will not work well as adults. Handling anger is a learned process like so many other processes we learned as we grew. Unfortunately, anger usually only gets addressed when we have a temper tantrum as an adult. Anger that gets buried inside also needs to be dealt with as it has the power to erupt.

Just because you are a grown up doesn't necessarily mean you are emotionally mature. Understanding your emotions and expressing them in a healthy way reflects wisdom.

Knowing how to express anger is a learned skill. Pay attention to your reaction and work toward an even-tempered response to anger. As an adult, maintaining your composure and self-control will look much better on you—and you will feel better too!

I say that trials and tests locate a person. In other words they determine where you are spiritually. They reveal the true condition of your heart. How you react under pressure is how the real you reacts.

John Bevere

You can control yourself if you really want to. I'll tell you how I know you can control yourself. If you were in a full-fledged emotional temper tantrum in your house and I knocked on your front door..... Come on! Let me tell you what, you would get control of yourself, and it would only take a few seconds.

Joyce Meyer

For Further Reflection

Ephesians 4:13–15; 1 Corinthians 13:11; Hebrews 5:12–14

TODAY'S PRAYER

Lord God, help me recognize my lack of growth and grant me grace as I mature. I pray for your help and wisdom in recognizing where I need help to be better in my responses to anger. Help me to express anger in a way that brings healing to me and to the situation. Amen.

Day 98

Blessings and Curses

*And so blessing and cursing come pouring out
of the same mouth. Surely, my brothers
and sisters, this is not right!*

JAMES 3:10

C ommunication is vital to relationships. What we say and how we say it affects the message we are trying to convey. When we are angry, sometimes the type of language we use changes. We say things in the moment that we regret later. Sometimes we use words we normally wouldn't. How can we make lasting changes in our communication, even when we are hot under the collar?

We have to address the built-up anger at the core. If you have the habit of verbally exploding when you are angry, it has become a release for you. Think about the last time you really got angry. What did you say? If you weren't mad would you use the same words? It's normal to feel angry sometimes, and it's healthy to release the frustrations and objections. However, if what you say when you are angry is hateful, demeaning, or attacking, you have to address the problem area that lies beneath the surface.

Choose to deescalate yourself in the moments when you would rather scream at the other person. Take time to deal with what is really going on inside of you. If you are in a relationship where lashing out at the other person is the typical communication, get help and begin to learn the power of a calm conversation.

The anger that is within us impacts the way we communicate with others. As you work on the anger inside of you, ask the Lord to provide you with the right words and the best attitude as you share what is on your mind. Your words are a barometer of what is happening in your heart. Make sure that what comes out of your mouth is an indication you are on the right path.

Never trust your tongue when your heart is bitter.

Samuel Johnson

The words of the tongue should have three gatekeepers: is it true? Is it kind? Is it necessary?

Arabian Proverb

The true test of a man's spirituality is not his ability to speak, as we are apt to think, but rather his ability to bridle his tongue.

R. Kent Hughes

For Further Reflection
1 Peter 3:10; Proverbs 13:3; Romans 15:6

TODAY'S PRAYER
Heavenly Father, help me control my tongue. Heal me of the anger that is beneath my outbursts and lead me to the pathway of peace. Guide me in every situation to reflect you in my conversations. Amen.

Contentment

*I know what it is to be in need, and I know what it is to
have plenty. I have learned the secret of being content
in any and every situation, whether well fed or hungry,
whether living in plenty or in want. I can do all this
through him who gives me strength.*

PHILIPPIANS 4:12–13 NIV

In this passage in Philippians, Paul talks about learning to
be content in all situations. That takes some work! When
you think of the things that irk, frustrate, or anger you,
how can you possibly be content? After all, some things just
are not OK and need to be corrected.

Anger can helps warn us of injustice and spur us to positive
action, when channeled correctly. If we get angry about
everything that goes wrong in our lives, we start focusing
on the frustrations, discontentment, and unhappiness.
Rather, we could be taking action to correct areas that need
improvement, accepting that life simply will not always go
the way we want. We must learn to control our anger and
focus our energy on making positive impact where we can
while at the same time learning to accept and be content with
situations that we can't change. Philippians 4:13 encourages
us that we will not have to do this hard work alone! We can
do all this through Christ who gives us strength.

What will your response be when life doesn't go your way?
Working toward contentment is a lifelong challenge. When
you're angry, you need God's help to change, make peace,

and right wrongs. The good news is that there is hope for you to experience contentment; it is possible to learn how to control your emotional reactions. The more you learn the stronger you will become and will be able to make a positive difference in the world!

It doesn't matter how strong your opinions are. If you don't use your power for positive change, you are, indeed, part of the problem.

Coretta Scott King

If you don't like something, change it. If you can't change it, change your attitude.

Maya Angelou

There is a certain relief in change, even though it be from bad to worse; as I have found in traveling in a stagecoach, that it is often a comfort to shift one's position and be bruised in a new place.

Washington Irving

For Further Reflection

Romans 15:5; Proverbs 4:23; Jeremiah 17:5

TODAY'S PRAYER

Lord, help me change my reactions to challenges and use difficulties to make positive change in my life. Help me grow in my contentment knowing that you are able to do more than I can ask or imagine in any situation. Amen.

Day 100

The Greatest is Love

Now we see things imperfectly, like puzzling reflections in a mirror, but then we will see everything with perfect clarity. All that I know now is partial and incomplete, but then I will know everything completely, just as God now knows me completely. Three things will last forever—faith, hope, and love—and the greatest of these is love.

1 Corinthians 13:12–13

Until you are with Jesus in heaven there will be things in life that will not make sense, bring discouragement and pain, and make you angry In those moments, remember what you have learned.

First, take a breath. If you pause when anger strikes, you will create a shift that can change the outcome in a positive way. Taking a breath provides the opportunity to respond in the best way possible and helps to re-center your thoughts and emotions.

Second, share what has angered you and release the emotion and feelings you are experiencing. The goal of communication is twofold: to not bury your anger inside, and to have a safe place to share. If you need to share deep pain and anger, do so with a supportive person who can help you navigate through the rage. If you need to share with your offender, create clear expectations regarding what would help you resolve the situation, or clarify that there is nothing that can be changed, but that you need to communicate your feelings. Remember how you communicate is vital.

Finally, understand that learning a new way of dealing with anger is a lifelong journey. In times of confusion, when life doesn't make sense and you feel anger, ask God to help you understand, accept, and know what to do.

God loves you and will always be there for you. Even when the hardest situations come your way, God is faithful and will make a way through.

If we have got the true love of God shed abroad in our hearts, we will show it in our lives. We will not have to go up and down the earth proclaiming it. We will show it in everything we say or do.

Dwight L. Moody

Learn to commit every situation to God and trust him for the outcome. God's love for you never changes, no matter what problems you face or how unsettled life becomes.

Billy Graham

For Further Reflections

John 3:16; Proverbs 10:12; 1 John 3:1

TODAY'S PRAYER

Lord Jesus, thank you for your love and grace! Help me continue to seek you daily. As I grow in your wisdom and grace, I am confident that you will work all things for the good. Thank you for the strength to follow you. You are worthy of praise! Amen.

DEVOTIONALS FROM
STEPHEN ARTERBURN

100 Days of Character Daily Devotional
Imitation Leather, 208 pages, 5" x 8"
ISBN: 9781628624953

100 Days of Prayer Daily Devotional
Imitation Leather, 208 pages, 5" x 8"
ISBN: 9781628624281

100 Days of Peace Daily Devotional
Imitation Leather, 208 pages, 5" x 8"
ISBN: 9781628624960

100 Days of Healing Daily Devotional
Imitation Leather, 208 pages, 5" x 8"
ISBN: 9781628624946

100 Days to Freedom from Fear and Anxiety
Daily Devotional
Imitation Leather, 208 pages, 5" x 8"
ISBN: 9781628629965

100 Days to Freedom from Depression
Daily Devotional
Imitation Leather, 208 pages, 5" x 8"
ISBN: 9781628629972